Style and Statement

Style and Statement

Edward P. J. Corbett
Robert J. Connors

New York • Oxford
Oxford University Press
1999

Oxford University Press

Oxford New York

Athens   Auckland   Bangkok   Bagota   Bombay   Buenos Aires
Calcutta   Cape Town   Dar es Salaam   Delhi   Florence   Hong Kong
Istanbul   Karachi   Kuala Lumpur   Madras   Madrid   Melbourne
Mexico City   Nairobi   Paris   Singapore   Taipei   Tokyo   Toronto   Warsaw

and associated companies in
Berlin   Ibadan

Published by Oxford University Press, Inc.,
198 Madison Avenue, New York, New York, 10016
http://www.oup-usa.org
1-800-334-4249

The content of *Style and Statement* is also published as Chapter IV, "Style" in the
fourth edition of *Classical Rhetoric for the Modern Student* by Edward P. J. Corbett
and Robert J. Connors, Oxford 1999.

Library of Congress Cataloging-in-Publication Data

Corbett, Edward P. J.
        Style and statement / Edward P. J. Corbett, Robert J. Conners.
            p.   cm.
        "Also published as Chapter IV, "Style," in the fourth edition of
    Classical rhetoric for the modern student, by Edward P. J Corbett and
    Robert J. Conners "
        Includes index.
        ISBN 978-0-19-511543-7
        1. English language—Rhetoric.   2. English language—Style.
    I. Connors, Robert J., 1951–   II. Title.
    PE1408.C5886   1999
    808'.042—dc21   97-26751
                                                               CIP

Printed in the United States of America
on acid-free paper

Contents

Preface

This book on style presents substantially the same treatment of style as the treatment in Chapter IV of the third and forth editions of *Classical Rhetoric for the Modern Student.* We discovered that many teachers of writing courses in the high schools and the colleges were spending more class time on the study of style than on any other chapter in the book. We surmised that the reason teachers were spending so much class time on this chapter was that the study of style offered more opportunities for students to engage in practical exercises than any other chapter in the book. So we decided to publish a separate book for those who were primarily or exclusively interested in the study of style.

Most contemporary students have had more exposure in school to the study of grammar than to style. In the Greek and Roman schools, the study of rhetoric consisted of five canons: (1) the discovery of arguments (Greek *heuresis;* Latin *inventio*); (2) the arrangement or organization of the arguments (Greek *taxis;* Latin *dispositio*); (3) the style, the verbalization, of the arguments (Greek *lexis;* Latin *elocutio*); (4) the memorizing of arguments (Greek *mneme;* Latin *memoria*); (5) the delivery of the arguments (Greek *hypokrisis*). The orator, of course, had to be in command of the language in which he delivered the speech, but if that delivery was to be effective, it had to be stylistically impressive. The style of the speech played a great part in persuading the listeners. The study of style was very important in the Greek and Latin schools of rhetoric. Style is also very important in the effectiveness of our written or spoken communication delivered in the English language.

As the contents in this book reveal, your study of style will be concerned with the kind of diction you use, the varying length of your sentences, the grammatical variety of your sentences, the euphony of your sentences, various ways in which you articulate the parts of your sentences, and the skillful and effective ways in which you use figures of speech. You will be made aware of many more kinds of figures of speech than you were aware of. The classical rhetoricians divided the study of the figures into two kinds: the schemes and the tropes. The schemes dealt with the deviation of the normal pattern or arrangement of words in a sentence; the tropes dealt with the deviation from the ordinary and principal kind of signification of words. You will also be exercised in the ways in which you can improve your own style. One of the exercises in this book is to copy, in handwriting, passages of prose written by some of the admired stylists in the English language. The mere copying of the sentences will acquaint you with the variety of ways in which you can express an idea or a feeling. Then you can write your own sentences, imitating the patterns of many of the sentences you copied.

The intensive study of style can significantly improve your own style and thereby make you a more effective communicator. Have fun playing with the language. And eventually that fun will make you a better writer and/or speaker.

June 1998   E. P. J. C.
                                                                                         R. J. C.

Style and Statement

The Study of Style

Style has been variously defined as the distinctive or characteristic way in which someone (1) dresses, (2) acts, (3) speaks or writes. In this book, we will be dealing with style as it relates to the way that someone speaks or writes. If someone writes "He don't care about anything." or "Has written she a letter the teacher." we say that both of those sentences are *ungrammatical*. The first one violates the rules of English grammar because of the wrong verb form, "don't care" instead of "doesn't care." The second sentence is grammatically faulty because of its word order. That English sentence would convey its meaning if it was written in the proper word order: "She has written the teacher a letter." This book will deal not so much with the grammar of the language as it will deal with the various ways in which someone might write or speak an English sentence. The first of the grammatically faulty sentences above would be stylistically acceptable if it was a sentence of dialogue in a story or a play. There are thousands of native speakers of English who would speak or write the sentence "He don't care about anything." And in a novel or a play that sentence would be an acceptable locution. In this book, we will be dealing with the various and acceptable ways in which we might say or write something.

The third part of classical rhetoric was concerned with style. Once arguments had been discovered, selected, and arranged, they had to be put into words. Words—either the sound symbols or the graphic symbols—serve as the medium of communication between speakers or writers and their audience. *Elocutio*, the Latin word for style, carried this notion of "speaking out." *Lexis*, the usual Greek word for style, carried the triple notion of "thought" and "word" (both of these notions contained the Greek word *logos*) and "speaking" (*legein*). The threefold implication of *lexis* indicates that the Greek rhetoricians conceived of style as that part of rhetoric in which we take the *thoughts* collected by invention and put them into *words* for the *speaking out* in delivery. Cardinal Newman's definition of style carried much the same idea: "Style is a thinking out into language."

It is this "thinking out into language" that presents the most formidable problem in composition for many students. The sight of a blank sheet of paper paralyzes them. It may be some comfort to such students to know that the transcriptions of words on a sheet of paper can be difficult even for professional writers. Writing never becomes easy; it just becomes easier. Alfred North Whitehead once said, "Style, in its finest sense, is the last acquirement of the educated mind; it is also the most useful." The difficulty that everyone has, in varying degrees, in putting thoughts into language stems partly from the inertia that must be overcome at the beginning of any task, partly from the lack of something to say, partly from indecisiveness about what to say first, and partly from the variety of possible ways to say something.

Inertia is a problem that can be overcome only by will power. One must simply sit down and resolve to write something on a piece of paper. Lack of things to say may be solved by the procedures discussed in the chapter on discovery of arguments. Indeciseness about the order of the parts may be resolved by attention to the suggestions presented in the chapter on arrangement. The problems posed by the fact that thoughts and feelings can be worded in a variety of ways will be the principal concern of this chapter.

One notion about style that needs to be erased at the outset is that style is simply "the dress of thought." It is difficult to determine just which school of rhetoric gave currency to the notion that style was ornament or embellishment, like the tinsel draped over the bare branches of a Christmas tree, but it is certain that none of the prominent classical rhetoricians—Isocrates, Aristotle, Demetrius, Longinus, Cicero, Quintilian—ever preached such a doctrine. All of these taught that there is an integral and reciprocal relationship between matter and form. "Thought and speech are inseparable from each other"—those words of John Henry Newman express the view of style that all the best rhetoricians held. According to this view, matter must be fitted to the form, and form to the matter.

This notion of the integral relationship between matter and form is the basis for any true understanding of the rhetorical function of style. It precludes the view that style is merely the ornament of thought or that style is merely the vehicle for the expression of thought. Style does provide a vehicle for thought, and style can be ornamental; but style is something more than that. It is another of the "available means of persuasion," another of the means of arousing the appropriate emotional response in the audience and of the means of establishing the proper ethical image.

If students adopt this functional notion of style, they will have gone part of the way toward solving some of their writing problems. They will begin to regard style in the way that Stendhal conceived of it: *Le style est ceci: Ajouter à une pensée donnée toutes les circonstances propres à produire tout l'effet que doit produire cette pensée* ("Style is this: to add to a given thought all the circumstances fitted to produce the whole effect which the thought is intended to produce"). Students will be guided in their choice of "the circumstances fitted to produce the whole effect" by a consideration of their subject matter, the occasion, their purpose, their own personality, and their audience. Jonathan Swift's definition of style as "proper words in proper places" is not much help to students until they have some criteria for deciding what is proper. The determination of what is proper can be arrived at only in relation to the above-named considerations.

Since *proper* is a relative term, there cannot be such a thing as an absolute "best style." A writer must be in command of a variety of styles, in order to draw on the style that is most appropriate to the situation. This is not to say that these several styles will differ radically from one another. Just as there is a common strain in the range of dialects that people command in their speech, so in their writing there will be a certain tenor that persists as they range from the most formal prose to the most relaxed prose. Each person, in other words, has an idiom—an idiom that is recognizable in all of his or her dialects and styles. The various styles will result from the variations that the writer or speaker works on this common tenor.

How do writers acquire the variety of styles needed for the variety of subject matter, occasion, and audience that they are bound to confront? The classical rhetoricians taught that a person acquired versatility of style in three ways: (1) through a study of precepts or principles (*ars*), (2) through practice in writing (*exercitatio*), (3) through imitation of the practice of others (*imitatio*). Rhetoric textbooks are concerned mainly with laying down the principles that will guide the student in acquiring effective styles. Practice and imitation are exercises that the student usually performs outside the classroom. For homework, the student is required to write themes; or the student may be asked to read "good writers," or to write a stylistic analysis of some writer, or to imitate passages of good writing.

Although this chapter will deal mainly with the precepts of effective writing, specimens of prose will be presented later for observation, analysis, and imitation. Practice in writing will have to come from the writing assignments set by the instructor, but at this point it is important to remind the student that practice in writing is the most beneficial of the three means. Precepts and imitation can *teach* the student how to write, but it is only by writing that the student will *learn* how to write. *One learns to write by writing.* Once is enough to enunciate that truism; but its truth cannot be recalled often enough.

With these few general remarks about style, we are ready to consider some of the precepts about style.

Grammatical Competence

In the study of style, we should be clear about the provinces of grammar and rhetoric. Just as the confusion between *grammar* and *usage* produced a great deal of needless controversy, so the confusion between *grammar* and *rhetoric* could hamper an intelligent discussion of the effective use of language. There are times, of course, when considerations of grammar will shade over into considerations of rhetoric. But while it is generally true that we must possess grammatical competence before we can develop an effective style, "good grammar" does not invariably produce "good rhetoric." Nor does "bad grammar" invariably produce "bad rhetoric." In April 1927, while awaiting execution in prison, Bartolomeo Vanzetti made this statement to a reporter:

> If it had not been for these thing, I might have live out my life, talking at street corners to scorning men, I might have die, unmarked, unknown, a failure. Now we are not a failure. This is our career and our triumph. Never in our full life can we hope to do such work for tolerance, for justice, for man's understanding of man, as now we do by an accident.

There are a number of errors in grammar and idiom in this utterance, but the passage has such a moving eloquence about it that it has become the most memorable statement to issue from the famous Sacco-Vanzetti case. Translated into flawless English, the utterance loses a great deal of its rhetorical effectiveness.

The smallest unit that falls within the province of rhetoric is the word. Unlike grammar, rhetoric is not concerned with *parts* of words, such as *morphemes* (the smallest segments that have meaning) and *phonemes* (those contrasting sound segments which enable a native speaker of the language to "hear" different words). It might be well at this point to set side by side the provinces of grammar and rhetoric:

GRAMMAR: phoneme–syllable–word–phrase–clause
RHETORIC: word–phrase–clause–paragraph–division–whole composition

It is clear from this schema that grammar and rhetoric overlap in the areas of the word, the phrase, and the clause. But although grammar and rhetoric deal with these common elements, their concern with these elements is not, strictly speaking, the same. Commonly we think of grammar as being concerned with "correctness" and of rhetoric as being concerned with "effectiveness." What we mean—or what we should mean—when we say that grammar is concerned with "correctness" is that grammar is preoccupied with how a particular language works—how words are formed and how words can be put together in phrases and clauses. What we mean when we say that rhetoric is concerned with "effectiveness" is that rhetoric deals with the choice of the "best" from a number of *possible* expressions in a language.

We can illustrate the difference by looking at an English sentence:

> He already has forgive them for leaving, before the curtain fell, the theater.

What the grammarian would pounce on here would be the word *forgive*. He or she would point out that modern English forms the perfect tense of the third-person singular verb with the auxiliary verb *has* and the past participle of the main verb. Once the grammarian had changed the verb in this sentence to *has forgiven*, he or she would have no more grammatical errors to correct in the sentence—that is, the grammarian would have to make no further changes in word order, inflections, or function words. But if the grammarians were to assume the additional role of the rhetorician, he or she would probably recommend further changes in the sentence. Although it is grammatically possible to place the word *already* and the clause *before the curtain fell* in the positions they now occupy in the sentence, it would be rhetorically advisable to alter the word order. The rhetorician would recommend that, in normal circumstances, the sentence read this way:

> He has already forgiven them for leaving the theater before the curtain fell.

The rhetorician would probably justify the changes in word order on the grounds that the sentence reads more naturally, more euphoniously, that way. There might be a rhetorical situation that would justify placing the adverb clause where it was in the original sentence, but it is difficult to imagine what that situation would be. On the other hand, it is easy to imagine a situation that would justify putting *already* at the head of the sentence. If, for instance, we wanted to emphasize the time element, we might say, "Already he has forgiven them. . . ."

Grammar would be concerned with the disposition of a word or clause only if the placement were impossible in English or would change the intended meaning of the sentence. English grammar would not permit this arrangement of words, for instance: *He has forgiven already them*. And if we were to say, "He had forgiven them before the curtain fell for leaving," the grammarian might ignore the awkward placement of the adverb clause but would have to point out that by such placement we have changed the meaning of the sentence: the adverb clause now modifies *had forgiven*; in the original sentence the adverb clause modified the gerund *leaving*.

Rhetoric and grammar are concerned, of course, with something more than just the placement of words, phrases, and clauses in a sentence, but this discussion of placement does illustrate the difference in the interest that grammar and rhetoric take in words.

Choice of Diction

An Adequate Vocabulary

Classical rhetoricians commonly considered style under two main heads: choice of diction, and composition of words in sentences. We will consider first the choice of diction.

In order to develop a good style, students must have, in addition to grammatical competence, an ample vocabulary. How do they acquire the rich vocabulary they need to develop a good style? There is no magic formula, certainly; the best advice that one can give students is to urge them to read at every opportunity. There is no doubt that persistent reading will add immeasurably to their vocabulary resources. Every English teacher is willing to testify that the best writing is usually done by those students who have been omnivorous readers. Not only do such students have more to say on any given subject, but they seem to have at their command the words they need to express what they have to say. We more easily remember the words that we encounter repeatedly in our reading. How we remember and recall words at the appropriate time is not known. But we do know that a person cannot give what he or she does not have. The person who reads a great deal is more likely to encounter new words than those who merely keep their ears open to the speech that is constantly swirling about them. The reason is that the vocabulary for impromptu talk and conversation is considerably more limited than the vocabulary for written prose.

Writers who have words ready when they need them are in a happy condition indeed. When apt words come readily, they know that they have gained command over words. They must feel something of the assurance displayed by the centurion in the New Testament: "I say to one, 'Go,' and he goes, and to another, 'Come,' and he comes." What is especially fortunate about such a verbal facility is that words that present themselves readily are likely to be the "proper words in proper places." When we have to strain for the *mot juste*, there is always the danger that the word finally chosen will be slightly awry.

So students who want to acquire an adequate vocabulary should heed the advice to read, read, read. But let them not trust solely to unconscious acquisition. Although they will absorb many new words merely by meeting them frequently, they will accelerate the assimilation of new words if they will take the trouble to look up the meaning of unfamiliar words as they meet them. As Henry James said, "Try to be one of the people on whom nothing is lost!" Students will be amazed at how quickly and solidly their vocabulary grows if they take the trouble to consult their dictionary every time they meet a new word.

Consulting the meaning of new words as one meets them is the best of the *conscious* methods of increasing one's vocabulary. It is best because it is functional: one is pursuing the meanings of words that one needs to know in order to understand what one reads.

There are other conscious ways to accelerate the acquisition of a rich vocabulary. One of these is to study lists of "new," "unusual," or "useful" words. We can add rapidly to our stock of words by such a systematic study of word-lists, and those who feel themselves to be notably deficient in vocabulary can expedite the catching-up process by learning and constantly reviewing a recommended list of words. There are many vocabulary exercises available, which students who want to add quickly to their knowledge of words would be well advised to consult.

Students should be warned, however, that this is the least satisfactory of the methods of vocabulary study. For one thing, they are studying words in isolation, not in a context. Studying words out of context can have a number of unfortunate consequences. First, knowledge of words tends to become an end in itself instead of a means. For another thing, the meaning of words studied out of context tend not to "stick" with the student as readily as they do when words are seen in the context of the reading that the student does. Any teacher who has subjected students to the study of selected word-lists knows how often he or she has been disappointed by seeing few of these words appear in the students' writing. The third consequence of studying words out of context is that students often use these words ineptly or unidiomatically. The student who writes, "George ate his chicken with hedonistic gusto," seems to be aware that *hedonistic* has some connection with sensuous pleasure but also reveals that he or she has not yet acquired the fine sense of knowing when words "fit." Nor does it help much to insist that students should compose a sentence using the word they have just looked up, because if they have not seen or heard the word used aptly they have no guide to its use. Students should not be discouraged, of course, from investigating the meanings of words that they find in some recommended list, because there is always some profit in such a pursuit, but students should be aware of the limitations of such an approach to words.

If writers have any reference tools on their desks, they are most likely to have a dictionary and a thesaurus. Writers often resort to their dictionary for spelling, for syllabication of words, for meanings of words. They do not resort to a thesaurus as often as they do to a dictionary, but it is the rare writer who has not sometime felt the need to consult a thesaurus. A thesaurus is indeed a valuable vocabulary-aid when the exact word that we need does not come to us readily.

The most famous thesaurus—the one that has become as much associated with synonymy as Webster is with lexicography and Bulfinch with mythology—is *Roget's Thesaurus of English Words and Phrases*, compiled originally by an English physician, Peter Mark Roget, and first published in London in 1852. Roget arranged his "treasury of words" under topical headings. Subsequent editors have revised the original *Thesaurus*, adding new words and removing some that had become obsolete, and the most recent editors have arranged the entries in alphabetical order to facilitate use. There are many inexpensive editions of *Roget's* available today, as well as other thesauruses prepared by modern editors. Students will find enough use for a thesaurus to warrant their buying a copy.

A thesaurus merely lists synonyms (and some antonyms) for the entry word, with cross-references to other entries. Since synonyms seldom if ever are identical in meaning, students need considerable knowledge of words and a fine discrimination to use a thesaurus intelligently. Suppose that a student is composing a paragraph describing the people who attended the opening of an opera season. In one of the sentences, she wants to convey the idea that the women who attended this event displayed a lack of taste and moderation in the way they dressed. She has written the sentence this way:

The ladies ostentatiously showed off their silks and satins and diamonds.

But she is not satisfied with the sentence. For one thing, she does not like the awkwardness of *showed off*. For another thing, she senses that there is something repetitious about *ostentatiously showed off* (doesn't *ostentation* mean "a show"?) Well, she will have to reword, perhaps recast, the sentence. If the new words or new phrases do not come to her immediately, she may find help in a thesaurus. But where does she start in the thesaurus?

Part of the difficulty in using a thesaurus is knowing just which entry one should consult. If one merely wants a substitute for a word, one has only to consult the entry for that word in the thesaurus. But sometimes one has an idea that one wants to convey, but no word for that idea suggests itself. In that case, one must conjure up some word or some concept (and it was here that Roget's original topical categories were helpful) that is close to the notion one wants to convey. Even a remote word will give the writer a starting point in the thesaurus. Synonyms for that word and cross-references to other words will move the writer closer to the exact word.

The student in our example is not sure, however, whether she needs just a substitute word or whether she needs an entirely new way of phrasing what she means to say. But since "showing off" is the general idea that she wants to convey with this sentence, she decides to start by consulting the entry *ostentation*. In *Roget's* she finds, as she will in most thesauruses, that the synonyms are grouped under part-of-speech headings—noun, verb, adjective, adverb. Looking at the list of synonyms under each part-of-speech heading may suggest to the student how to reword or revise her sentence. She would like to keep, if she can, the "silks and satins and diamonds" of her present sentence because these words are concrete and sensory. (Perhaps without knowing it, the student has produced the figure of synecdoche—the material here standing for the thing made from it.) From the nouns listed under *ostentation*, she experiments with various combinations:

> The ladies made a *display* (or *show, flourish, parade*) of their silks and satins and diamonds.

Perhaps adding the adjective *vulgar* (or *garish, gaudy, glittering*) would reveal her value judgment on the scene—would, in other words, reveal her attitude toward the scene:

> The ladies made a vulgar display of their silks and satins and diamonds.

Then she experiments with some verb combinations suggested by the synonyms listed under *ostentation*: *to exhibit, to display, to parade, to flaunt, to prink, to primp*. She finally settles on the verb *flaunt*—

> The ladies flaunted their silks and satins and diamonds.

—because *flaunt* combines all the notions and attitudes that she tried to convey in her original sentence; and *flaunt*, being concrete and picturesque, fits well with the figure of speech that follows it.

A thesaurus can be a valuable aid when "the proper word in the proper place" does not immediately present itself. But students should be on their guard against the temptations offered by such a treasury. Those who have gone through a period of serious effort to improve their style may recall how difficult it was at times to resist the temptation to replace all the drab, ordinary words with some of the resplendent, polysyllabic words discovered in a thesaurus. A student, for instance, might compose a sentence like this:

> After the fire had been put out, the police roped off the street and prevented all sightseers from strolling past the charred ruins.

But that is too lackluster, he tells himself. So mining his lexicographical lode for some sesquipedalian nuggets, he bedizens his humdrum sentence in this fashion:

> After the conflagration had been extinguished, the police obstructed the thoroughfare and forefended all inquisitive spectators from perambulating before the incinerated residue of the pyrogenic catastrophe.

Fortunately, students who persist in their efforts to improve their style eventually outgrow their penchant for such polysyllabic anfractuosities. Perhaps the price that one has to pay for an enriched vocabulary is a period of addiction to "big" words. The ordeal will inflict no permanent damage if the students can "kick the habit" in its early stages.

Purity, Propriety, and Precision of Diction

So far in our discussion of diction we have touched on two qualifications that students must have if they are to improve their style: they must know the grammar of the language, and they must have an adequate vocabulary. Our concern from this point on will be mainly with the *rhetorical* competence that students must have to make wise choices among words. George Campbell pointed up the distinction between grammatical and rhetorical competence in this way: "the grammatical art bears much the same relation to the rhetorical which the art of the mason bears to that of the architect."

The prime quality of prose style is *clarity*—or, to use the sonorous Latinate term, *perspicuity*. Since the object of rhetorical prose is persuasion, it follows that such prose must communicate with those who are to be persuaded. And if rhetorical prose must communicate, it follows that it must, above all, be clear. As one might expect from the person who viewed rhetoric as an activity that always involved an audience, Aristotle held that "language which does not convey a clear meaning fails to perform the very function of language." Lord Macaulay, one of the masters of the limpid prose style, put it this way: "The first rule of all writing—that rule to which every other is subordinate— is that the words used by the writer shall be such as most fully and precisely convey his meaning to the great body of his readers."

Clarity comes from selecting words carefully and arranging them well. Leaving aside the problem of arrangement for now, how can writers learn to select the proper words? They will be helped in making the selection by keeping three criteria in mind—purity, propriety, and precision. While some judgments about whether language is pure, appropriate, and precise can be made only when writers see words in a sentence and when they view them in relation to their subject, purpose, and audience, it is still possible to say something about the purity, propriety, and precision of isolated words.

The discussion of *purity of diction* involves us, willy-nilly, in a consideration of those much-maligned criteria that George Campbell set forth in the eighteenth century to determine "good usage." In order to merit the stamp of approval, words must be, according to Campbell, in *reputable* use, in *national* use, and in *present* use. Despite the relativity of these criteria, there would seem to be little practical difficulty in using at least two of the criteria—national use and present use—to help us determine whether our diction is "pure" and therefore clear. If we are to communicate with a contemporary audience, it stands to reason that we must use current words and idioms—that is, words and idioms, however "old" they may be, that are understood by people today. Likewise, we must use the words that have a national currency. This criterion demands that we avoid dialectical words, technical words, coinages, and foreign words. But this second criterion immediately calls for some qualification. If we view words in relation to an audience, for instance, we see that there are some situations that call for localisms, technical jargon, neologisms, and even foreign words.

When we try the third criterion, reputable use, we run into more difficulty. Campbell proposed this standard for judging reputable locutions: "whatever modes of speech are authorized as good by the writings of a great number, if not the majority, of celebrated authors." But is it conceivable that in a modern pluralistic society we could ever arrive at any consensus about who our "celebrated authors" are? Moreover, if two "celebrated authors" are in conflict on a matter of usage, which author do we follow?—the one who is *more* celebrated? And is it possible for the ordinary educated person to determine in every case, or even in many cases, whether a certain locution is sanctioned by a "great number" or "the majority" of celebrated authors?

These practical difficulties lead many people to rely on some arbiter of usage. The best source of such guidance is a reference work that boldly claims to be an arbiter. Fortunately, there are a few esteemed dictionaries of usage available. These dictionaries offer reliable guidance because the men or women who prepared them had good taste in language to start with and refined their taste with a close study of actual usage.

The most famous of these reference words is H. W. Fowler's *A Dictionary of Modern English Usage*, first published in 1926 but many times reprinted. This book has become a bible of usage for many famous writers and editors. Fowler was himself a lexicographer, having compiled, with the help of his brother Francis George Fowler, *The Concise Oxford Dictionary*. To his sound knowledge of the English language, Fowler added a discriminating taste, and he wrote with such grace and wit that he was himself an exemplar of the "good English" that he advocated. It was Fowler who assured us, once and for all, that it was permissible at times, even advisable, to split an infinitive or to end a sentence with a preposition. And he made household words of some of the headings in his alphabetically arranged dictionary—tags like Battered Ornaments, Cannibalism, Elegant Variation, Out of the Frying Pan, Sturdy Indefensibles.

Students will have to consult *A Dictionary of Modern English Usage* to discover for themselves the value and flavor of this admirable reference work. But here is a taste of Fowler's wit and judgment, taken from his article on the subject we have just been discussing—purity of diction:

> PURISM. Now & then a person may be heard to 'confess', in the pride that apes humility, to being 'a bit of a purist'; but *purist* & *purism* are for the most part missile words, which we all of us fling at anyone who insults us by finding not good enough for him some manner of speech that is good enough for us. It is in that disparaging sense that the words are used in this book; by *purism* is to be understood a needless & irritating insistence on purity or correctness of speech. Pure English, however, even apart from the great numbers of elements (vocabulary, grammar, idiom, pronunciation, & so forth) that go to make it up, is so relative a term that almost every man is potentially a purist & a sloven at once to persons looking at him from a lower & a higher position in the scale than his own. The words have therefore not been very freely used; that they should be renounced altogether would be too much to expect considering the subject of the book. But readers who find a usage stigmatized as purism have a right to know the stigmatizer's place in the purist scale, if his stigma is not to be valueless. Accordingly, under headings of various matters with which purism is concerned, a few articles are now mentioned illustrating the kind of view that may be expected in other articles of a similar nature: . . .
>
> From H. W. Fowler, *Dictionary of Modern English Usage*, Oxford University Press, pp. 474–75. Copyright © 1965 by the Clarendon Press, Oxford University Press. Reprinted by permission.

With the passage of time, Fowler's dictionary was bound to become outdated—at least on some matters of usage. And as the gap between British English and American English widened, American writers began to see that Fowler was not relevant to some of the locutions that had developed in the United States.

To fill the need for an up-to-date dictionary of usage that would pay special attention to American English, the Oxford University Press in 1957 published Margaret Nicholson's *A Dictionary of American-English Usage*. In her Preface, Miss Nicholson announces that her book is an adaptation of, not a replacement for, Fowler's *MEU*. She has retained many of Fowler's long articles, has abridged others, and has added a number of her own entries on modern Americanisms.

In 1965, the Clarendon Press published a revised edition of *A Dictionary of Modern English Usage* by Sir Ernest Gower. Now the Clarendon Press at Oxford has in the works a completely new edition of Fowler's *A Dictionary of Modern English Usage*.

In 1957, Bergen Evans and Cornelia Evans published a completely new dictionary of American usage, *A Dictionary of Contemporary American Usage* (Random House). Writers who are loyal to Fowler will continue to use *due to* only in adjectival structures (*His absence was due to sickness*, but not, *The government failed due to widespread discontent with its policies*). But those writers who have come to trust the painstaking study that the Evanses have made of actual usage will probably be guided by this statement about the present status of *due to*:

> *due to* may be used to qualify a noun, as in *a mistake due to carelessness*. This use of *due to* was limited by Dr. Johnson as "proper, but not usual." Since then it has become a familiar form of speech and no one thinks of objecting to it. But the words are also used today to qualify a verb, as in *he failed, due to carelessness*. This construction is relatively new and is condemned by some grammarians.
>
> In both cases the words *due to* are being used as *owing to* might be used. It is claimed that *due to* is acceptable in the first case but not in the second, and that only the form *owing to* may be used with a verb. This distinction cannot be defended on theoretical grounds, since *due to* and *owing to* are grammatically alike. The critics usually content themselves with saying that "*due to* cannot be used to qualify a verb." But it is used to qualify a verb, millions of times every day. And it is used in this way in very respectable places. A tablet in front of the Old State House in Philadelphia reads: *Here the Continental Congress sat from the date it convened, May 10, 1775, until the close of the Revolution, except when, in 1776–77, it sat in Baltimore, and in 1777–78, in Lancaster and York, due to the temporary occupation of Philadelphia by the British army*. (See also *owe*.)
>
> From Bergen Evans and Cornelia Evans, *A Dictionary of Contemporary American Usage*. Copyright © 1957. Reprinted by permission of Random House Inc.

Any of the three dictionaries of usage we have discussed would be a valuable addition to your library. If your dictionary does not settle your doubts about the "purity" of a certain expression, a dictionary of usage can be of real help to you. You should be cautioned, however, not to develop a neurotic concern about usage. If American schools had been as much concerned with grammar, logic, and rhetoric, as they have been with "good usage," the quality of student writing today might be better than it generally is.

The principal point to be emphasized about purity of diction is that one's language must be intelligible and acceptable to an audience. There will always be a certain level of diction below which a speaker or writer will never slip, however crude and unlettered the audience may be. There is a large stock of words, a reservoir of "basic English," that will always be intelligible and acceptable to any audience. Deviations from this basic stock of ordinary words will be governed mainly by the nature of the audience addressed.

Propriety or appropriateness is the quality of diction that can least be judged in isolation; it always implies a judgment made in relation to something else. Conceivably, we could look at isolated words and make some judgment about whether they were current or national or reputable, but it is impossible to judge the appropriateness of isolated words.

Diction is appropriate when it suits our subject matter, our purpose, the occasion, and the audience. Unfortunately, there are no handbooks that can help you make judgments about the appropriateness of your diction. Everyone seems to be endowed with a certain minimal sense of appropriateness— a sense absorbed from the experience of living in a society. Instinctively, we "tone up" our everyday language when we shift from a situation in which we are addressing our peers and intimates to a situation in which we are addressing, say, the dean of the college. We make similar adjustments in our diction as our subject matter, occasion, and purpose change.

The refinements of this minimal sense of appropriateness will come naturally, as our experience deepens and our education advances, and will develop in proportion to our native intelligence and our conscious efforts to improve this sense. Just as certain people seem to inherit and develop a superior ability to get along with other people, so some of them develop a keener sense than others for the appropriateness of their language.

Involved in this matter of appropriateness are the connotations of words. When we are concerned with the purity or precision of diction, we are concerned mainly with the denotations of words—with the dictionary meanings of verbal symbols. But in our choice of appropriate diction we must also take into consideration the connotations of words—those emotional and tonal qualities that come to be associated with words. We cannot control the connotations that cluster around a word; we can only be aware of those connotations and take advantage of them. It makes a great difference whether we call a person a "politician" or a "diplomat." Because of the connotations that attend these words, the first word will tend, with most audiences, to dishonor the person, while the second word will tend to honor him or her.

The connotations of words have great rhetorical value—for example, in promoting the emotional appeal of a discourse. Robert H. Thouless has ably demonstrated the emotional value of connotations in his analysis of the diction in two verses by John Keats:

> In *The Eve of St. Agnes*, Keats has written:
>
> > Full on this casement shone the wintry moon,
> > And threw warm gules on Madeline's fair breast.
>
> These are beautiful lines. Let us notice how much of their beauty follows from the proper choice of emotionally colored words and how completely it is lost if these words are replaced by neutral ones. The words with strikingly emotional meanings are *casement, gules, Madeline, fair,* and *breast. Casement* means simply a kind of window with emotional and romantic associations. *Gules* is the heraldic name for red, with the suggestion of romance which accompanies all heraldry. *Madeline* is simply a girl's name, but one calling out favorable emotions absent from a relatively plain and

straightforward name. *Fair* simply means, in objective fact, that her skin was white or uncolored—a necessary condition for the colors of the window to show—but also fair implies warm emotional preference for an uncolored skin rather than one which is yellow, purple, black, or any of the other colors which skin might be. *Breast* has also similar emotional meanings, and the aim of scientific description might have been equally well attained if it had been replaced by such a neutral word as *chest*.

Let us now try the experiment of keeping these two lines in a metrical form, but replacing all the emotionally colored words by neutral ones, while making as few other changes as possible. We may write:

> Full on this window shone the wintry moon
> Making red marks on Jane's uncolored chest.

No one will doubt that all of its poetic value has been knocked out of the passage by these changes. Yet the lines still mean the same in external fact; they still have the same objective meaning. It is only the emotional meaning which has been destroyed.

> From Robert H. Thouless, *How To Think Straight*, Holder and Stoughton
> Ltd., Copyright 1932 by Robert H. Thouless.

You are probably well aware by now that poets exploit the emotional values of words, but you may not always be alert to the subtle emotional effects exerted by connotation in a prose text. Faced with the evidence of H. L. Mencken's scholarly three-volume study of American English, you would have to concede that he had a profound knowledge of his native language, but perhaps you would not be sufficiently aware of how he manipulated the connotations of words to effect his rhetorical purpose. Consider this example in which Mencken is seeking to influence our attitude toward a certain kind of teacher:

> Such idiots, despite the rise of "scientific" pedagogy, have not died out in the world. I believe that our schools are full of them, both in pantaloons and in skirts. There are fanatics who love and venerate spelling as a tomcat loves and venerates catnip. There are grammatomaniacs; schoolmarms who would rather parse than eat; specialists in an objective case that doesn't exist in English; strange beings, otherwise sane and even intelligent and comely, who suffer under a split infinitive as you or I would suffer under gastro-enteritis. There are geography cranks, able to bound Mesopotamia and Baluchistan. There are zealots for long division, experts in the multiplication table, lunatic worshipers of the binomial theorem. But the system has them in its grip. It combats their natural enthusiasm diligently and mercilessly. It tries to convert them into mere technicians, clumsy machines.

> From H. L. Mencken, "Pedagogy," *A Mencken Chrestomathy*, New York:
> Alfred A. Knopf, 1949, p. 305. Reprinted by permission of the publisher.

We cannot examine all the techniques that Mencken uses in his satirical writings, but we can note here the subtle way in which he influences our reactions simply by his choice of words. A good deal of the effect of this passage is produced by Mencken's "name-calling." The "names" that Mencken used here are heavily freighted with emotional overtones—*idiots, fanatics, schoolmarms* (one of Mencken's favorite derogatory epithets), *cranky, zealots, lunatic worshipers*. All of these words carry the discrediting connotation of extreme, irrational commitment to a cause—the taint of "enthusiasm" that many critics ascribed to the evangelical sects in eighteenth- and nineteenth-century England. Where Mencken fails to find an emotional epithet to suit his purpose, he invents one—*grammatomaniacs*. Most readers do not know what *gastro-enteritis* means; but they do not have to know—the word just *sounds* awful. Notice how Mencken, in the second sentence of this passage, indicates that he is talking about both men and women teachers—"in pantaloons and in skirts." *Pantaloons* was an especially clever choice. *Pants* would have been the word that most of us would have chosen as the counterpart of *skirts*. But Mencken detected the extra connotative value of the word *pantaloons*, suggesting to a modern audience something archaic, slightly feminine. Note too how Mencken uses a simile in the third sentence to depreciate the object of his satire, comparing devotees of correct spelling to the lowly, back-alley *tom-cat*. One of the deadliest words in the English language is the word *mere*. Mencken uses this word with devastating effectiveness at the end of this passage, where he begins to shift his ground of attack, warning us that these "enthusiastic" pedagogues are now in danger of being turned into dispassionate machines as a result of their exposure to "teachers' college" bunkum. What is more chilling than to be called a "mere technician"?

We see then that the connotations of words must be considered in any judgment about the appropriateness of diction. Sensitivity to the connotations of words cannot be taught; it must be learned. What is even harder for the student to acquire is a fine sense for knowing how far to go in exploiting the emotional force of connotations. Mencken perhaps goes too far in the passage we have just considered. In most of his satirical writings, he relied too heavily on the shock technique that derived from the use of hyperbolic, simplistic diction. Many people are alienated rather than persuaded by his intemperate language. Clever writers can sometimes be too clever for their own good. It does not take a sledge-hammer to drive a nail.

We turn now to the third quality, precision. The word *precision* has its roots in the Latin verb *praecidere*, "to cut off." A precise word is a word shorn of all superfluous and irrelevant notions, a word that signifies neither more nor less than we intend to say. Words may be dubbed "imprecise" (1) when they do not express exactly what we intended to say; (2) when they express the idea but not quite fully (3) when they express the idea but with something more than we intended.

If we write, "I was pleased by his fulsome praise," we may not have said what we intended to say. If we consult the dictionary meaning of *fulsome* ("disgusting or offensive, mainly because of its excessiveness or insincerity"), we will see how wide of the mark we have come. If we write, "I thought it was a tremendous performance," we convey the general idea that we approved of the performance, but we convey no exact notion of the particular way in which this performance was "tremendous." If we write, "As a result of examining the basic flaws in the situation, he came up with a radical solution to the problem," we choose an apt word in *radical* (a solution that gets at the *root* of the problem), but unwittingly we suggest an additional meaning that we did not intend (a solution that is *wild* or *subversive*). A word then will be inexact if it expresses *too little* or *too much* or if it is *too general*.

It is perhaps better to discuss faulty idiom here than under the head of pure diction, because, like the diction cited in the previous paragraph, faulty idiom "misses the mark." The reason why lapses in idiom constitute one of the commonest faults in student writing is that idiom, like connotation, is one of the tricky aspects of language. Dictionaries and handbooks of usage will more often be helpful to you in matters of idiom than in matters of connotation, but your most reliable guide to correct idiom is your own awareness of how your native language is spoken. Those who have not read very much or who have not kept their ears open to the turns of phrase are the ones most likely to violate the idiom of the language.

The "turns of phrase" in the previous sentence suggests an important observation about idiom. No single word, considered in isolation, can be declared unidiomatic. If we say of a certain word, "Native speakers of the language do not use that word," we are saying simply that such a word does not exist in the English language. A word can be classified as unidiomatic only in relation to some other word or words. No one could say of the word *for* that it is unidiomatic; either it is an English word or it is not. *For* can become unidiomatic only when it is used in conjunction with another word, as with the word *unequal*, in the sentence, "The judge proved to be unequal for the task." Then we can point out that native speakers of the language do not use the preposition *for* with *unequal*; they say "unequal *to* the task."

What complicates the difficulty is that grammar is of no help to the student in deciding matters of idiom. There is nothing ungrammatical in the locution "unequal for the task." Idiom is a matter of usage rather than of grammar: native speakers just do not say "unequal for." Neither is logic of much help to the student in regard to idiom. When we say, for instance, "He *looked up* the word in the dictionary," we are, in a sense, violating logic, because when we consult a word in the dictionary, we are more likely to *look down* the page to find the word than to *look up* the page. But "look up a word" is the correct idiom simply because that is the way people say it.

Sometimes the prefixes of words will provide a clue to the idiomatic preposition that goes with those words. So we say, "he *de*parted *from* the scene," "the crowd *e*merged *from* the stadium," "he *is ad*verse *to* the proposal," "they *com*pared it *with* the first version," "the station-wagon *col*lided *with* the motorcycle," "he *ab*stained *from* all alcoholic beverages." But the lexical meaning of these Latin prefixes is not always a clue to the proper preposition, for we also say, "in *con*trast *to*" (as well as "in *con*trast *with*"), "he *de*parted *for* the station," "she *com*pared him *to* an overgrown bear."

Since neither grammar nor logic is a reliable guide to proper idiom, we must develop our own awareness of the peculiar way in which native speakers of the language say certain things. Perhaps the last proficiency we acquire in learning a foreign language is a sense for the idioms of the language. It is a commonplace that the best way to attune our ear to the idioms of a foreign language is to live for a time in a community where that language is spoken exclusively. So in learning the idioms of our own language, we must *listen* to the speech that is all about us, and we must carefully observe the turns of phrase in the contemporary prose we read. Teachers can point out lapses in idiom and can correct the faulty idiom in your writing, but in the absence of any "rules" about idiom, you must develop your own sense for the idiosyncrasies of expression. You must become aware not only of the proper idiom but of the subtle changes of meaning and tone affected by idiom. In an article on the idiomatic preposition, John Nist has illustrated some of the vagaries of idiom:

> Doting grandparents may indulge in loving pride and make *over* a favorite one-toothed blue-eyed darling. But a pouting lover had better make *up with* his sweetheart first; his chances of making *out* are otherwise very slim. An imbiber can conceivably be sleeping *in* while sleeping *out* for the sole sake of sleeping it *off*. How many a long-suffering son-in-law has had a run *in* with her whose kiss is colder than a mackerel because he intended to *run out* on his wife by running *off with* the understanding secretary? One of the favorite maxims of chilly age for flaming youth goes like this: Be careful how you live it *up*; you may never live it *down*! A philosopher chews *upon* a difficult thought; an able prosecutor chews *up* the defense attorney's arguments; a catcher chews *over* the signals with his pitcher; a diner chews *around* the bone; and an angry man chews *out* his offensive neighbor. A cut*up* at the party may cut *out* from the stag line and cut *in* on the belle of the ball. And he who goes all *out* in tracking down the tricky idiomatic preposition will undoubtedly find himself all *in*.

> From John Nist, "The Idiomatic Preposition." By permission. From a December issue of Word Study © 1963 by Merriam-Webster Inc., publisher of the Merriam-Webster dictionaries®.

Many other observations might be made about diction, such as that diction should be "natural," "vigorous," "concrete," "graceful," "harmonious," but these epithets merely represent alternate ways of saying that diction should be *pure, appropriate*, and *precise*. Besides, our judgments about the naturalness, vigor, concreteness, gracefulness, and harmony of diction—or, to use our own terms, the purity, propriety, and precision of diction—can best be made when we view diction in the context of a sentence and in relation to our rhetorical purpose. There will be times, for instance, when it might suit our purpose to make our diction awkward or insipid or abstract or ugly or unmusical.

In summary: Since words are the building-blocks of our sentences, it is obvious that we must have an adequate supply of words to erect the kind of edifice we have planned. When our supply of words is low, we will have to make some effort to add to our stock. Our working vocabulary will naturally expand as our experience and education expand, but we can accelerate the expansion by reading a great deal and by consulting dictionaries and thesauruses. Since we seek to communicate with others, it stands to reason that our diction must first of all be intelligible—intelligible, that is, to a particular audience. It will be mainly the audience that will determine whether we can use learned words or technical terms or foreign words or slang. The audience, the subject matter, the occasion, and our purpose constitute the criteria for judging the appropriateness of our diction. In addition to choosing intelligible and appropriate diction, we must choose diction that is as precise as the situation permits and demands. Dictionaries and handbooks of usage will help solve some of our problems with usage, idiom, and connotation, but we will have to depend mainly on the development of our own sensitivity to these aspects of language.

Composition of the Sentence

Words are symbols of ideas, but they do not begin to "say" anything until we put them together. Sentences, which are syntactical units composed of words, "say" something, partly because of the *lexical content* (the meaning) of the words and partly because of the *grammatical forms* that govern words put together in patterns. Up to this point, we have been speaking mainly about the lexical aspect of words. As we move now to a discussion of the composition of the sentence, we must begin to be concerned with syntax. Eventually, we will be led into a discussion of another aspect of language: how the *rhetorical forms* of sentences, the schemes, constitute a third carrier of meaning.

As we pointed out in the previous section on choice of diction, no one can begin to develop a style until he or she has a basic competence in the grammar of the language. We presume that the student has this basic competence and is thus ready to develop the rhetorical competence he or she needs to compose effective sentences.

Rhetorical competence plays its part in the writing process when there are choices to be made from among two or more grammatical possibilities. Stylistic variations in the syntax of the sentence cannot ignore the grammar of the language. Any changes we make must be grammatical.

As a starting point for our discussion of the rhetoric of the sentence, let us take this minimal sentence:

> The boy loves the girl.

Native speakers of the language recognize this as a pattern of words that make a statement. They know the meanings of the words, and they are familiar with the grammar of the sentence: the function word *the*, the inflectional concordance between the subject and predicate, and the word order. Anyone who wanted to make a statement, in the English language, about a young male of the human species having a certain emotional attitude toward a young female of the human species would be limited in the words that could be chosen to express this idea and even more severely limited in the way these words could be put together to say what was intended. As far as *rhetoric* goes, there is very little we could do with this sentence. We might make some different choice of words—proper nouns to preface the *boy* and *girl* or a synonymous verb to replace *loves*—to make the sentence rhetorically more effective. But there is almost nothing we could do to alter the grammar of the sentence. We cannot say "Boy love girl" or "Loves the boy the girl." No, we must dispose whatever words we choose in the usual pattern for a statement—subject-verb-complement (S-V-C)—and use the proper inflectional forms.

It is when we begin to expand this minimal sentence pattern that rhetoric has a bearing. There are a number of ways in which we can expand this sentence, and within each of the various ways there are often alternatives. Once there are alternatives, there are choices to be made; and once choices are to be made, rhetoric comes into the picture.

One of the ways in which we can expand our minimal sentence is by adding single-word, phrasal, or clausal modifiers to the *head word* in the S or V or C. For instance:

The tall, handsome boy sincerely loves the short, homely girl.

Can we alter the order of any of these modifiers? Yes, we can make *some* changes—changes that are grammatically and idiomatically possible but not always stylistically advisable. For example, we could make these changes:

The boy, tall and handsome, loves sincerely the short, homely girl.

Rarely does one see adjectival single-word modifiers placed *after* the head word in the complement: . . . *sincerely loves the girl, short and homely.* The following order is also possible in English:

Tall and handsome, the boy loves the short, homely girl sincerely.

We might choose this order, for instance, if we wanted to emphasize the boy's tallness and handsomeness and the sincerity of his love for the girl.

Another way to expand the minimal sentence is to use prepositional phrases as modifiers of any one or all of the head words in the S-V-C pattern:

The boy from Montana loves, with uncommon fervor, the girl from Missouri.

Prepositional phrases used as adjectival modifiers are almost always placed *after* the noun or pronoun they modify. There are some instances, however, when the prepositional phrase used adjectivally will be placed *before* the noun that it modifies. For example,

About this development, he had been given no advance warning.

(Here the phrase *about this development* modifies *warning*.)

Prepositional phrases used adverbially have more freedom of movement than do prepositional phrases used adjectivally. There are three other places where the phrase *with uncommon fervor* could be placed in our sentence:

> With uncommon fervor, the boy from Montana loves the girl from Missouri.
>
> The boy from Montana loves the girl from Missouri with uncommon fervor.
>
> The boy from Montana with uncommon fervor loves the girl from Missouri.

There are a number of other ways in which we could expand our minimal sentence:

1. compounding the head words in the S-V-C pattern;
2. juxtaposing appositives to the head words in the S-V-C pattern;
3. using verbals or verbal phrases (participles, gerunds, and infinitives) in the S-V-C pattern;
4. using noun clauses to serve as the S or the C in the S-V-C pattern;
5. using adjective clauses to modify the S or C head word in the S-V-C pattern;
6. using adverb clauses to modify the V in the S-V-C pattern.

We could go on to illustrate these methods of expanding the sentence and to investigate the alternatives (if any) in word order of each of these methods, but we can pursue these matters in the structural and transformational grammars now available. This brief excursion into the syntax of the English sentence serves to give a general idea of what we mean by the rhetoric of the sentence.

When we are presented with a number of syntactical choices, all of them grammatically and idiomatically possible, we will elect the possibility that best serves our purpose at the moment. If, for instance, one of the possibilities allows us to put a word or phrase in an emphatic position and if emphasis of that word or phrase is what we want at that point, then we should take advantage of that possibility. There are times when we want to de-emphasize a word or phrase, and in that case we should elect that possibility which would bury the word or phrase somewhere in the interior of the sentence. We might elect another grammatical possibility on the grounds that this disposition of words improved the rhythm of the sentence. Sometimes we might reject a grammatical possibility because it lends itself to ambiguity. (Such a case would be the "squinting modifier" in the sentence "The band-master strutted along *boldly* twirling a baton.") And of course we sometimes elect a grammatical possibility for no other reason than that we want to avoid monotony of sentence structure.

There is another point to be made here about the rhetoric of the sentence. Style, like grammar, is part of the expressive system of a language. Just as grammatical devices, like word order and inflections, are carriers of meaning, so the forms of sentence—the *schemes*, as the Renaissance rhetoricians called them—are expressive of meaning too. For example, let us consider the rhetorical device of parallelism. When we have to express a series of similar or equivalent "meanings," we usually resort to the grammatical device of compounding, and we reinforce the co-ordinate value of the compounded elements with the rhetorical device of parallelism.

We can illustrate how parallelism can be expressive of meaning by looking at a sentence in which it is a pronounced feature:

> He [the president of a large, complex university] is expected to be a friend of the students, a colleague of the faculty, a good fellow with the alumni, a sound administrator with the trustees, a good speaker with the public, an astute bargainer with the foundations and the federal agencies, a politician with the state legislatures, a friend of industry, labor, and agriculture, a persuasive diplomat with donors, a champion of education generally, a supporter of the professions (particularly law and medicine), a spokesman to the press, a scholar in his own right, a public servant at the state and national levels, a devotee of opera and football equally, a decent human being, a good husband and father, an active member of a church.

> From Clark Kerr, *The Uses of the University*. Copyright © 1963.
> Reprinted by permission of Harvard University Press.

This is an unusually long sentence, but it is so well articulated that it conveys its meaning clearly. The expansion, all of which takes place in the complement part of the sentence, is managed with a series of parallel structures. The student could learn the whole art of parallelism from a close study of this remarkable sentence. An analysis of the sentence reveals several levels of parallelism and enough variation in the basic pattern to break an otherwise monotonous rhythm. The basic pattern is this:

indefinite article	*noun*	*prepositional phrase*
a	friend	of the students
a	colleague	of the faculty

Dr. Kerr varies the rhythm of this basic pattern in several ways: (1) by introducing an adjective before the noun ("a good fellow with the alumni"); (2) by throwing in an adverb ("a champion generally"); (3) by inserting a parenthesis ("particularly law and medicine"); (4) by compounding the objects of the preposition ("a friend of industry, labor, and agriculture") or by compounding the adjectives modifying the object of the preposition ("a public servant at the state and national levels").

The main point that we want to make about this sentence, however, is that the rhetorical form is one of the carriers of meaning. The theme of Dr. Kerr's essay is that the modern university has become so huge and complex that it can no longer be regarded as a *uni*-versity but must be regarded now as a *multi*-versity. The point he is making in the section of the essay from which the above sentence was taken is that the president of such a multiversity must wear many hats, must be many things to many people. In this sentence he is enumerating some of the capacities in which the president is expected to serve, using a series of phrases. This compounding (without conjunctions, for the most part) is one of the expressive devices for indicating the variety of roles the president must play. But because Dr. Kerr also wants to indicate that the president is expected to play each of these roles equally well he uses the device of parallelism, which serves to reinforce the co-ordinate value of these several capacities. Dr. Kerr does not expect his reader to remember all these roles; he wants only to convey the general impression of the heavy burden that the president carries. Incidentally, the *length* of the sentence has a rhetorical function too: the long cataloguing is weighty and exhausting to the reader, as the job is to the president.

In the next sentence but one, Dr. Kerr makes use of antithesis, another rhetorical device, to convey the notion of the contrary qualities that the president must combine in his personality. Here is that sentence of 114 words:

> He should be firm, yet gentle; sensitive to others, insensitive to himself; look to the past and the future, yet be firmly planted in the present; both visionary and sound; affable, yet reflective; know the value of a dollar and realize that ideas cannot be bought; inspiring in his visions yet cautious in what he does; a man of principle yet able to make a deal; a man with broad perspective who will follow the details conscientiously; a good American but ready to criticize the status quo fearlessly; a seeker of truth where the truth may not hurt too much; a source of public pronouncements when they do not reflect on his own institution.

> From Clark Kerr, *The Uses of the University*. Copyright © 1963. Reprinted by permission of Harvard University Press.

The various levels of parallelism and antithesis in this sentence look like this when laid out schematically:

```
He   should be   firm   /   yet gentle
                 sensitive      /        insensitive
                      to others               to himself
        look                           /  yet be firmly planted
            to the past and the future                      in the present
                      both visionary  /  and sound
                      affable  /  yet reflective
            know the value of a dollar  /  and realize that ideas cannot be bought
                      inspiring            /  yet cautious
                          in his visions            in what he does

                      a man            /  yet able
                          of principle              to make a deal
```

(antithesis persists, but parallelism is violated: a noun, *man*, yoked with an adjective, *able*; *man* modified by

prepositional phrase but *able* modified by infinitive
phrase)

a man
    with broad perspective
    who will follow the details conscientiously

(again the antithesis is in the words—*broad perspective /
details*—rather than in the structure)

a good American / but ready
                to criticize the status quo fear-
                lessly

(departure from parallelism again)

a seeker
    of truth
        where the truth may not hurt too much

a source
    of public pronouncements
        when they do not reflect on his own institution

As we will make clear when we come to discuss the figures of speech, the
rhetoricians commonly associated the various schemes and tropes with the
topics of *logos, pathos*, and *ēthos*. Antithesis, for instance, was tied up with
the topic of dissimilarity or with the topic of contraries. In the third book of
his *Rhetoric*, Aristotle pointed out the value of antithesis in discourse: "Such
a form of speech is satisfying, because of the significance of contrasted ideas
is easily felt, especially when they are thus put side by side." Whether Dr.
Kerr was aware of the theory of antithesis is immaterial. What is important
is that by putting his "contrasted ideas" in juxtaposition, he has assisted the
communication of his meaning.

Up to this point we have been concentrating on only a few stylistic features—word order, methods of expansion, parallelism, antithesis. It is time
now to consider a broader range of stylistic features, not only so that we can
get to know what these various features are and how they function but so
that we can derive the maximum benefit from the exercises in imitation later
on in the chapter and can incorporate some of these features into our own
style.

Study of Style

Before you can benefit from a close observation of stylistic features, you
must have some technique for analyzing prose style. Because you have
spent little or no time analyzing prose style, you may not know what to
look for in sentences and paragraphs. You have undoubtedly been im-

pressed by the style of certain prose writers, but you are almost tongue-tied when asked to point out what it is you particularly admire about their style. The best you can do is to characterize various styles with such general, subjective epithets as "clear," "crisp," "urbane," "orotund," "whimsical," "heavy," "flowing," "staccato." The New Criticism gave students a technique and a terminology for analyzing poetry, but most students do not know where to begin if they are asked to analyze the style of a piece of prose.

First, let us set down, in outline form a list of features that you can look for when analyzing prose style.

A. Kind of diction
    1. general or specific
    2. abstract or concrete
    3. formal or informal
    4. Latinate (usually polysyllabic) or Anglo-Saxon (usually monosyllabic)
    5. common words or jargon
    6. referential (denotative) or emotive (connotative)
B. Length of sentences (measured in number of words)
C. Kinds of sentences
    1. grammatical: simple, compound, complex, compound-complex
    2. rhetorical: loose, periodic, balanced, antithetical
    3. functional: statement, question, command, exclamation
D. Variety of sentence patterns
    1. inversions
    2. sentence openers
    3. method and location of expansion
F. Means of articulating sentences (coherence devices)
G. Use of figures of speech
H. Paragraphing
    1. length (measured in number of words and number of sentences)
    2. kind of movement or development in paragraphs
    3. use of transitional devices

Most of the items in this outline represent features that lend themselves to objective study. Some of the either/or combinations under "Kind of diction" are relative, and opinions about them could vary. But most of the features lend themselves to objective study in the same way that grammatical features (word order, inflections, function words) do. There are a number of incalculable features of style about which we might never be able to secure general agreement, but if we are to develop any system for analyzing prose style we must start with those features that are objectively observable.

Kind of Diction

The kind of diction that a writer habitually uses can tell us a great deal about the quality of the writer's mind and style. We made the point earlier that a writer must be in command of several styles, so that he or she can accommodate his or her manner to various subject matters, occasions, purposes, and audiences. But even within this range of styles, there will be a certain persistent level of style associated with that author. Dr. Johnson and Oliver Goldsmith displayed their versatility by trying their hands at several literary genres, but whether they were writing poems or plays or novels or familiar essays or critical essays, they maintained a certain note that identified the style as their own and no one else's. That peculiar note was achieved partly by the kind of diction they used: Johnson's philosophical, polysyllabic, Latinate diction; Goldsmith's concrete, familiar, colloquial diction. The "weight" of a person's style can be measured partly by the syllabic composition of the words. The "tone" of a person's style can be measured partly by the texture of the words—their phonic values, their relative abstractness or concreteness, their level of usage. Judgments about the formality or informality of a person's style are made largely on the basis of the level of diction used.

Length of Sentences

The average length of sentences also can lead to some valid generalizations about a person's style. Modern prose style is characterized by sentences that are generally shorter than those of earlier centuries. (The narrow columns into which journalistic prose is fitted undoubtedly had some influence on the shortening of the sentence.) But we still discover remarkable variations in sentence-length in modern writers. We can arrive at a tenable generalization about a writer's characteristic sentence-length by counting the words in, say, five hundred consecutive sentences and then dividing the total number of words by the number of sentences. Having determined this average sentence-length, we would have to pursue the more important consideration: what relation does this characteristic sentence-length have to the rhetorical situation?

Kinds of Sentences

Some very interesting observations can be made about a person's style and habits of thought by studying the kinds of sentences used and the proportions in which the various kinds are used. W. K. Wimsatt, for instance, in his valuable study *The Prose Style of Samuel Johnson*, saw in Dr. Johnson's persistent use of parallel and antithetical clauses a reflection of the bent of his mind: "Johnson's prose style is a formal exaggeration—in places a caricature—of a certain pair of complementary drives, the drive to assimilate ideas, and the drive to distinguish them—to collect and to separate." And so Dr. Johnson disposed his collection of ideas in parallel structures; he reinforced the distinctions in ideas by juxtaposing them in antithetical structures.

The history of the prose style of most Western languages reveals a gradual evolution from a paratactic syntax—stringing together a series of coordinate structures without conjunctions—to the most sophisticated of sentence patterns, subordination. In Anglo-Saxon, for instance—the earliest extant record of the English language—we note the lack of the relative pronoun and the subordinating conjunction, two of the grammatical devices by which Modern English renders clauses dependent. When we catalogue the kinds of grammatical sentences found in modern professional prose, we find surprisingly few compound sentences. Modern writers expand their sentences more by subordination and apposition than by compounding. Observation of the grammatical kinds of sentences can tell us a great deal about someone's prose style and can point up significant deficiencies in our own prose style.

Variety of Sentence Patterns

A study of variety in sentence patterns also has some valuable lessons to teach us about style. For one thing, such a study can dispel many of the myths about prose style. It is true that professional writers command a greater variety of lexical and syntactical resources than unpracticed writers do, but they do not make a fetish of variety for its own sake. Professor Francis Christensen made a study, for instance, of sentence-openers in the first 200 sentences of some narrative and expository works written by modern American writers. Here are the results of his findings in the expository pieces:

Expository	Sentence Openers	Adverbial	Verbal	Inverted	Co-ord. Conj.
Carson, *Sea Around Us*	79	74	4	1	29
M. Chute, *Shakespeare of London*	64	63	0	1	4
De Voto, *Easy Chair*	51	50	1	0	16
Edman, *Arts and the Man*	37	33	2	2	14
Highet, *Art of Teaching*	47	45	2	0	22
Mencken, *Vintage Mencken*	72	67	5	0	9
Lloyd & Warfel, *American English*	77	72	4	1	4
Thrilling, *Liberal Imagination* (pp. 216–34)	60	57	3	0	34
Van Doren, *Shakespeare; Four Tragedies*	32	32	0	0	29
Wilson, *Literary Chronicle:* 1920–1950 (pp. 9–29, 422–27)	56	51	3	2	14
TOTAL	575	544	24	7	175
PERCENTAGE	28.75	27.20	1.15	0.40	8.75

From Francis Christensen, "Notes Toward a New Rhetoric· I Sentence Openers," *College English,* 25 (October 1963) 9. Copyright 1963 by the National Council of Teachers of English. Reprinted with permission.

The numbers in the first column indicate the number of sentences, among the 200 studied in each piece, that had sentence openers (words, phrases, or clauses which are not part of the subject cluster); the numbers under the next four columns mark the various kinds of sentence openers. Rachal Carson had the highest percentage of sentence openers (39.5 percent); Mark Van Doren had the lowest percentage (16 percent). But the combined percentages show that almost three-quarters of the sentences written by these authors started out with the subject cluster rather than the sentence openers and that almost 95 percent of the 575 sentence openers were of the adverbial type.

These figures would seem to indicate that some of our esteemed modern writers do not, contrary to common opinion and to the advice given in some writing texts, strive for a notable variety in the ways they begin their sentences. And the figures also invalidate the prescription about not beginning a sentence with a co-ordinating conjunction. Descriptive studies of other aspects of prose as it is actually written would probably destroy some additional illusions about how professional writers create their effects.

Sentence Euphony

Prose rhythm is one of the most difficult aspects of style to analyze. Perhaps the closest thing we have to the elaborate prosody that the Greeks and Romans devised for their quantitative languages is the system for scanning the English sentence that George Saintsbury worked out in his *A History of English Prose Rhythm* (Edinburgh, 1912). The euphony and rhythm of sentences undoubtedly play a part in the communicative and persuasive process—especially in producing emotional effects—but students would be ill advised to spend a great deal of time learning a system for scanning prose sentences. Euphony and rhythm are largely a matter for the ear, and students would do just as well to read their prose aloud to catch awkward rhythms, clashing vowel and consonant combinations (as in that five-word phrase), and distracting jingles. If, for instance, the student who wrote the following sentence had read it aloud, he or she might have caught the distracting repetition of the *ect* sound: "I will show how the testimony affected some people indirectly connected with the selection of the jurors." It is probably more important to apply this test when one is preparing a discourse for oral delivery, but most good writers apply this test also to prose that they know will be read silently. The sentence that is difficult to enunciate is often a grammatically or rhetorically defective sentence.

But if writers are not confident about relying on their ears for testing the rhythm of their sentences, they can resort to the fairly simple method of marking the stresses in series of words. With a little more ingenuity, they might be able to group the stressed and unstressed syllables into feet. In scanning poetry, we can get by with knowing the five most common feet in classical prosody: iambic (˘ –), trochaic (– ˘), anapaestic (˘ ˘ –), dactylic (– ˘ ˘), and spondaic (– –). To scan prose, however, we need a great many more combinations. In her book, *The Anatomy of Prose*, Marjorie Boulton defines 23 different combinations, which constitute, she says, "all the possible feet used in English prose." (Students who want to pursue these technicalities can consult pp. 55–57 of her book.) To illustrate this system of scansion, here is the way that Miss Boulton scanned the first nine verses of Psalm 90 in the Authorized Version of the Bible:

Lord, thou/ has been/ our dwelling place/ in all generations./

Before/ the mountains/ were brought forth,/ or ever/ thou hadst formed/ the earth/ and the world,/ even/ from everlasting/ to everlasting,/ thou art God./ .

Thou turnest man/ to destruction;/ and sayest,/ Return,/ ye children/ of men./

For a thousand/ years in/ thy sight/ are but/ as yesterday/ when it is past,/ and as a watch/ in the night./

Thou carriest/ them away/ as with a flood;/ they are as a sleep:/ in the morning/ they are like grass/ which groweth up./

In the morning/ it flourisheth,/ and groweth up;/ in the evening/ it is cut down,/ and withereth./

For we are consumed/ by thine anger,/ and by thy wrath/ are we troubled./

Thou hast set/ our iniquities/ before thee,/ our secret sins/ in the light/ of thy countenance./

For all/ our days/ are passed/ away/ in thy wrath;/ we spend/ our years/ as a tale/ that is told./

Miss Boulton goes on to say about this passage: "My stresses will not, I think, be disputed much, though even on this point some ears might object; many readers will probably disagree with the division into feet at some point. However, we can now see the contrast of stressed, monosyllabic endings and lighter endings, with the finality of the stress at the end on a heavy monosyllable. We see how the important words are also placed where, with their own strong senses, they are surrounded by weak stresses to make them stronger by contrast. We may also notice, if we are beginners, that the four-syllable and five-syllable feet are needed to describe prose accurately."

Articulation of Sentences

An investigation of the ways in which writers articulate their sentences can be one of the most fruitful exercises for students who want to improve the quality of their own prose. Coherence is a troublesome problem for most students. They usually develop a sense for unity and emphasis long before they master coherence. Cultivating the habit of thinking in an orderly, logical fashion is the best way to insure that they will express their thoughts coherently. But practiced writers use a number of linguistic devices to assist the coherent display of their thoughts. Let us see how an accomplished writer like Matthew Arnold makes his prose "hang together." Some of the verbal devices he uses to promote coherence are italicized; others will be pointed out in the commentary afterward.

> The critical power is of lower rank than the creative. *True*; but in assenting to *this proposition, one or two things* are to be kept in mind. It is undeniable that the exercise of a *creative* power, that a free *creative* activity, is the highest function of man; *it* is *so* by man's finding in it his true happiness. *But* it is undeniable, *also*, that men may have the sense of exercising *this free creative activity* in *other* ways than in producing great works of literature or art; if it were not *so*, all but a very few men would be shut out from the *true happiness* of all men. *They may have it* in well-doing, *they may have it* in learning, *they may have it* even in criticising. *This* is *one thing* to be kept in mind. *Another* is that the exercise of the *creative* power in the production of *great works of literature or art*, however high *this* exercise of *it* may rank, is not at all epochs and under all conditions possible; *and* that *therefore* labour may be vainly spent in attempting *it*, *which* might with more fruit be used in preparing for *it*, in rendering *it* possible. *This creative power* works with elements, with materials; what if *it* has not *those materials*, those *elements*, ready for *its* use? *In that case, it* must surely wait till *they* are ready.
>
> From Matthew Arnold, "The Function of Criticism at the Present Time," *Essays in Criticism*, First Series, 1865.

Most coherence devices (pronouns, demonstrative adjectives, repeated words and phrases, and some of the conjunctions) point backwards to what has just been said, thus connecting what has been said with what is about to be said. One of the commonest devices in Matthew Arnold's prose—so common, in fact, that it has become a distinctive mark of his style—is the frequent repetition of key words and phrases. Arnold was a great phrasemaker, and once he had coined a phrase that carried the theme of an essay, he repeated that phrase time and time again in the essay. So conspicuous was this mannerism in his prose that one is inclined to believe that the cardinal principle of his expository technique was the famous pedagogical maxim, "Repetition is the mother of studies." The most obtrusive repetition in this selection is the word *creative*—the key word of this paragraph and one of the two key words in the entire essay. The repetition then of substantive words is one of the linguistic means of stitching our sentences together.

Arnold also frequently uses demonstrative pronouns and demonstrative adjectives (*this, that; these, those*) and personal pronouns. The original meaning of the word *demonstrate* is "to show, to point." Demonstrative pronouns and adjectives usually point backwards, tying what follows to what has gone before. By their very nature, all pronouns (except indefinite pronouns, like *anyone* and *someone*) point to a referent. Because of the close relationship between the pronoun and its referent, it is extremely important to be sure the referent is clear. When it is vague or, worse yet, when the referent is not there at all, the coherence of our writing is bound to suffer.

Good writers also make liberal use of conjunctions and conjunctive adverbs for stitching sentences together. The chief grammatical function of co-ordinating conjunctions is to splice together words, phrases, and clauses. But when co-ordinating conjunctions are placed at the beginning of the sentence (and Professor Christensen's chart reveals how often modern writers use sentence-openers), these conjunctions assume the rhetorical function of providing a logical bridge between sentences. Conjunctive adverbs—words like *however, nevertheless, moreover, also, indeed, therefore*—are even more common devices for aiding coherence. One can point up the logical relationship between sentences simply by inserting the appropriate conjunctive word.

We will note only two additional devices that Arnold uses to connect his sentences. Fragmentary sentences can sometimes strengthen coherence. We have an instance of this in the second sentence of Arnold's paragraph. The single word *True* constitutes an elliptical sentence. Filled out, the ellipsis would read something like this: "That proposition is true." The single word here conveys a meaning only because of its juxtaposition to the previous sentence; since it has to look backward to the previous sentence in order to become meaningful, it is "tied" to that sentence. This same principle of "dependent meaning" prevails in conversation, where we often talk in fragmentary sentences ("Where are you going tonight?" "The movies." "With whom?" "Charlotte.").

Another device that Arnold uses in this paragraph is parallelism, which is reinforced by the figure of anaphora (repetition of identical words at the beginning of successive phrases). Three independent clauses are set down, one after the other ("They may have it in well-doing, they may have it in learning, they may have it even in criticising"). Although there are no conjunctions (asyndeton) to tie the clauses together grammatically, the clauses are connected by parallel structure and identical words. In addition to the functions that we noted in the analysis of Clark Kerr's two sentences, parallelism can also be used for coherence.

The passage quoted from Matthew Arnold exemplifies most of the verbal devices that good writers use to articulate their sentences. Good writers use such devices so unobtrusively that the sutures hardly show. A study of how an author uses them will help to account for the clarity of one person's prose and the fuzziness of another's.

Figures of Speech

Since we are going to devote a long section of this chapter to a discussion of figures of speech, this is not the place to discuss them in detail. Suffice it to say here that they constitute one of the most revealing features of a person's prose style. If they are apt and fresh, they can contribute greatly to the clarity, liveliness, and interest of one's style. But they must not be cultivated for their own sake. The excessive, strained use of figures proved to be detrimental to the "gracefulness" for which the Euphuistic writers of the sixteenth century were striving in their prose. On the other hand, the absence or scarcity of figurative language can have a deadening effect on style. Although it is not true that Jonathan Swift excluded all figurative language from his prose, it is true that he used figurative language sparingly. That rarity of metaphorical language may have been what Dr. Johnson had in mind when he made his famous comment on Swift's style: "For purposes merely didactic, when something is to be told that was not known before, [his style] is in the highest degree proper, but against that inattention by which known truths are suffered to lie neglected, it makes no provision; it instructs, but does not persuade."

Paragraphing

There is a style of paragraphing as well as a style of sentence structure. Paragraphing, like punctuation, is a feature only of the written language. As a matter of fact, we can regard paragraphing as a typographical device for punctuating units of thought larger than the thought conveyed by a single sentence. We are so accustomed to seeing, in the print we read, indentations of segments of thought that we come to take paragraphing as much for granted as we do the left-to-right movement of printed words. And because the indentations are always there on the printed page, we do not realize how much the marking off of thought-units facilitates our reading. Perhaps the best way to show how typographical devices contribute to the readability of printed prose is to reproduce a passage of prose with no punctuation, capitalization, or paragraphing:

> it seems to me that it was far from right for the professor of english in yale the professor of english literature in columbia and wilkie collins to deliver opinions on cooper's literature without having read some of it it would have been much more decorous to keep silent and let persons talk who have read cooper cooper's art has some defects in one place in deerslayer and in the restricted space of two thirds of a page cooper has scored 114 offenses against literary art out of a possible 115 it breaks the record there are nineteen rules governing literary art in the domain of romantic fiction

some say twenty two in deerslayer cooper violated eighteen of them these eighteen require that a tale shall accomplish something and arrive somewhere but the deerslayer tale accomplishes nothing and arrives in the air they require that the episodes of a tale shall be necessary parts of the tale and shall help to develop it but as the deerslayer tale is not a tale and accomplishes nothing and arrives nowhere the episodes have no rightful place in the work since there was nothing for them to develop they require that the personages in a tale shall be alive except in the case of corpses and that always the reader shall be able to tell the corpses from the others but this detail has often been overlooked in the deerslayer tale

If we have difficulty making sense out of this river of words, we should be grateful to those printers and grammarians who invented typographical devices to mark off meaningful segments of thought. After trying out various combinations, we might eventually be able to make sense of this passage, especially in those sections where there are enough grammatical signals to tell us what words are related. We will probably make faster progress in deciphering the passage if we read it aloud, because the voice will add another grammatical element, intonation, which is the vocal equivalent of the graphic marks of punctuation. But there will be spots in this passage that will remain ambiguous, because grammar will allow in those places two or more combinations of words, each of which would make sense.

Now let us reproduce the passage as Mark Twain wrote it, restoring his punctuation, capitalization, and paragraphing:

It seems to me that it was far from right for the Professor of English in Yale, the Professor of English Literature in Columbia, and Wilkie Collins to deliver opinions on Cooper's literature without having read some of it. It would have been much more decorous to keep silent and let persons talk who have read Cooper.

Cooper's art has some defects. In one place in *Deerslayer*, and in the restricted space of two-thirds of a page, Cooper has scored 114 offenses against literary art out of a possible 115. It breaks the record.

There are nineteen rules governing literary art in the domain of romantic fiction—some say twenty-two. In *Deerslayer* Cooper violated eighteen of them. These eighteen require:

1. That a tale shall accomplish something and arrive somewhere. But the *Deerslayer* tale accomplishes nothing and arrives in the air.

2. They require that the episodes of a tale shall be necessary parts of the tale and shall help to develop it. But as the *Deerslayer* tale is not a tale, and accomplishes nothing and arrives nowhere, the episodes have no rightful place in the work, since there was nothing for them to develop.

3. They require that the personages in a tale shall be alive, except in the case of corpses, and that always the reader shall be able to tell the corpses from the others. But this detail has often been overlooked in the *Deerslayer* tale. . . . [Twain goes on to designate, in a series of short, numbered paragraphs, the remaining fifteen "rules."]

From Mark Twain, "Fenimore Cooper's Literary Offenses," 1895.

The typographical device that contributes most, of course, to clarifying the syntax of a succession of words is the device for marking off sentences—an initial capital letter and end-punctuation (period, question mark, exclamation point). We underestimate, perhaps, how much of a contribution to clarity is made by other typographical devices—such simple things as commas, capital letters, italics, hyphens, quotation marks. Nor should we overlook the contribution that indentation of paragraphs makes to ease of reading. The value of paragraphing is evident in the Mark Twain passage. Indentation marks the shifts in the development of thought and indicates the relationship of the parts. Simply by setting off the violated rules in separate paragraphs and further marking them with numbers, Mark Twain makes it clear that he is specifying a series of parts.

A study of the density of an author's paragraph tells us a great deal about the "weight" of his or her style. Many considerations, of course, dictate whether paragraphs will be long or short—the subject matter, the occasion, the audience. Narrative, for instance, especially when it is dealing with rapid action, often moves along in a series of short paragraphs. In dialogue, too, each shift of speaker is indicated by a new paragraph. For purposes of transition or emphasis, an author will insert a one- or two-sentence paragraph. And if we are writing copy for the narrow columns of a newspaper, we will rather arbitrarily chop up our prose into very short paragraphs.

But when all allowances have been made for such conventions and for various rhetorical situations, it remains true that professional writers generally write longer paragraphs than unpracticed writers do. Many of the one- and two-sentence paragraphs that students write have no rhetorical justification whatever. Such short paragraphs simply reveal that the students have not developed their thoughts adequately. They have nothing more to say, or think they have nothing more to say, on the idea presented in that paragraph. Perhaps by resorting to the topics to find something to say, students will be able to put some meat on the bare bones of their paragraphs.

A Student Report on a Study of Style

We have devoted several pages to a discussion of the objectively observable features of style because it is by this kind of close analysis that one learns why the style of an author produces its effects and learns also how to go about improving one's own style. To illustrate the profit to be derived from such a close study, we will present the results of a student project.[*]

Two sections of an Honors Freshman class were set the task of making a comparative analysis of the length of sentences and paragraphs in a specified number of paragraphs in F. L. Lucas's essay "What Is Style?" and in all the paragraphs of one of their expository themes. For the purposes of this study,

[*]For an account of similar projects devised for an Advanced Composition course at the University of Nebraska, see Margaret E. Ashida and Leslie T. Whipp, "A Slide-Rule Composition Course," *College English*, XXV (October, 1963), 18–22.

a sentence was defined as "a group of words beginning with a capital letter and ending with some mark of end-punctuation." The students were told that in choosing eight paragraphs from the Lucas essay they should avoid short transitional paragraphs and any paragraphs containing two or more sentences of quoted material. The students were presented with a mimeographed sheet containing the following items to be filled in:

EVALUATION	PROFESSIONAL	STUDENT
A. Total number of words in the piece studied	_____	_____
B. Total number of sentences in the piece studied	_____	_____
C. Longest sentence (in no. of words)	_____	_____
D. Shortest sentence (in no. of words)	_____	_____
E. Average sentence (in no. of words)	_____	_____
F. Number of sentences that contain more than 10 words *over* the average sentence	_____	_____
G. Percentage of sentences that contain more than 10 words over the average	_____	_____
H. Number of sentences that contain 5 words or more *below* the average	_____	_____
I. Percentage of sentences that contain 5 words or more below the average	_____	_____
J. Paragraph length		
longest paragraph (in no. of sentences)	_____	_____
shortest paragraph (in no. of sentences)	_____	_____
average paragraph (in no. of sentences)	_____	_____

The numbers that the students entered in the first column differed according to the paragraphs they chose to study, but we can give some mean figures for four of the items in the list:

1. The average length of Lucas's sentences was 20.8 words.
2. About 17 percent of Lucas's sentences were ten words or more over the average.
3. About 40 percent of Lucas's sentences were five words or more below the average.
4. Lucas averaged 7.6 sentences per paragraph—a fairly well-developed paragraph.

Most of the students found that their average sentence matched the length of Lucas's average sentence. Many of the students were surprised to learn, however, that they had a higher percentage of above-average sentences and a strikingly lower percentage of below-average sentences. Perhaps the most dramatic difference that the students noted was in paragraph development. At least half of the students found that they were averaging between three and four sentences in their paragraphs.

In addition to filling out the mimeographed sheet, the students submitted an essay in which they commented on what they had learned about style from this exercise. Excerpts from their essays are reproduced below.

First of all, here are some of the students' comments about sentence length and sentence variety:

> I found that the percentage of sentences in Lucas's essay that contained more than ten words over the average sentence was 17%, while mine was a mere 3%. But the percentage of his sentences that contained five words or more below the average was 39% compared to my 16%. I see now that I must strive for greater variety of sentence structure and length in my themes in order for the pieces to be more effective.
>
> . . . . .
>
> My average sentence length is very close to that of Mr. Lucas. I think this is misleading, however, since in my high school newspaper work I acquired the habit of gathering more than one thought in a single sentence. My sentence length is good, but my sentence content could be improved. Another factor that was evident is that I tend to use fewer short sentences than professional writers do. I think I can explain this lack of short sentences by considering the subject matter of the themes I write. I have noticed that in the past I would use longer, more involved (and less clear) sentences to write about things I didn't feel completely at ease in writing about. I use short sentences to present ideas that are very lucid to me.
>
> . . . . .
>
> One thing I found is that good prose doesn't necessarily imply long verbose sentences and polysyllabic words.
>
> . . . . .
>
> There is not quite enough variety in length or pattern in my sentences. Even my longer sentences tend to be of the compound variety rather than the complex or compound-complex type.

Now for some excerpts from students' comments on paragraphing:

> This paragraph analysis revealed some drastic differences in style. My paragraphs, surprisingly, are considerably longer than Lucas's. The average number of sentences per paragraph in my work is twelve, whereas Mr. Lucas's average is about eight. My longest paragraph has sixteen sentences, twice the professional's average. This could indicate poor paragraph planning and division on my part. My extended paragraphs seem much like run-on sentences and probably have a tiring effect on my reader.
>
> . . . . .
>
> My longest paragraph is 17 sentences, almost 10 sentences over my average paragraph length; Lucas's longest paragraph has 10 sentences, less than 3 sentences over his average paragraph length. Also, in this long paragraph the average length of sentences is 14 words, which is 7 words per sentence below the average for the whole theme. And in this same paragraph of mine there are 12 out of the total 17 sentences which contain 5 words or more below the average sentence. The reason for this paragraph being strikingly different from my average paragraph is that I used a different

style of writing in this paragraph. I tried to make an emotional appeal to back up my arguments, using short questions and terse statements. In trying to give the effect of an impassioned speech, I departed from my usual prose style; thus this paragraph is not representative of my usual style of paragraphing.

. . . . .

In Lucas's piece there is an average of 126 words per paragraph, while I have an average of only 70 words per paragraph. I probably should use more words to develop my ideas, not for the sake of wordiness but for the sake of being more fully understood. I leave out examples and explanations which may be vital to the clarity of the theme.

. . . . .

In the paragraphs I chose to study, Mr. Lucas used a total of fifty-six sentences. I used a total of fifty-four sentences in my theme. This averages to approximately seven sentences per paragraph in both essays. However, this similarity is slightly invalid. In choosing the Lucas paragraphs, I was careful to choose only those which were of an "average" length; I purposely skipped those paragraphs which seemed short. One of the paragraphs in my theme contained only three sentences, but I had to count it. This tended to lower my average number of sentences per paragraph, whereas Mr. Lucas's average was slightly inflated because only "average" paragraphs were studied.

. . . . .

Another thing that I realized when doing this stylistic study is that in the professional writers' work the paragraphs fit together like the pieces in a jigsaw puzzle. Each paragraph develops a separate thought but becomes an integral part of the whole. I have trouble tying my ideas together. Although all my ideas relate to the theme topic, often I find that they do not follow in a logical pattern.

In addition to commenting on sentences and paragraphs, several students commented on other features of style that they had noted in doing this study. Here are some excerpts from those comments:

I see now that enlarging my vocabulary is necessary to improve my style. I don't mean necessarily that I must start using bigger words; I mean rather that I must learn when certain words should be used. I must learn to use big words only when they fall naturally into place and when they can be fully understood by the intended audience. Professional writers do not always use big words, but their knowledge of words enables them to use the proper word at the proper time.

. . . . .

One characteristic of Lucas's style which I don't like and which I think I avoided in my writing is the excessive use of parentheses and dashes. I certainly feel that a parenthesis or a dash is appropriate at times, and, in fact, I used a dash four times in my writing. But I believe that Mr. Lucas over-worked parentheses and dashes. I feel that the reader's train of thought is broken when the writing contains many dashes or parentheses.

. . . . .

Lucas brings his writing to life by the use of figures of speech. When he says, "Men are often taken, like rabbits, by the ears," his writing becomes vivid and distinctive. Another of Mr. Lucas's figures of speech, "There are blustering signatures that swish across the page like cornstalks bowed be-fore a tempest," shows that he avoids the trite, overworked figures. He searches for new and fresh expressions. I noticed that in my piece of writ-ing there wasn't a single simile, metaphor, or personification.

. . . . .

Although Lucas's longest sentence is twice as long as my longest sentence, my sentence is harder to follow. This difference in readability can be at-tributed partly to the number of syllables. Although syllable-count was not included on the study sheet, it has a great bearing on the clarity of one's prose. The majority of words in Lucas's sentences are monosyllabic. Be-cause of the monosyllabic diction, the interest of the reader is not bogged down by heavy words.

. . . . .

This study also confirmed something I was already suspicious of—I don't write really long sentences. This, I believe, is due to the fact that I am afraid of the punctuation a long sentence may require. It is much simpler to write two short sentences correctly than to write one long sentence cor-rectly. Since we were graded in high school more on correctness than on style, I formed the habit of writing two shorter sentences rather than one long one. I guess I'll have to start worrying about style as well as correct-ness if I want to become a good writer.

. . . . .

I noticed how well the parts of Mr. Lucas's essay were proportioned and how mine seemed rather top-heavy. A closer look showed me that I overdevelop the beginnings of my essays, often leaving the middle thinly developed.

. . . . .

I have noticed that sometimes my sentences sound artificial and stiff be-cause I place adverb clauses and verbal phrases where they do not fit natu-rally. . . . Good professional writers have mastered the art of appropri-ateness. I have found that most professional writers' long sentences are surprisingly easy to follow, while my long sentences are frequently too in-volved to be understood.

. . . . .

Here are a few excerpts from the students' comments on the general value of a close study like this. What is practically notable is that the students retained their sense of perspective. They saw no merit in cultivating any feature of style for its own sake; a stylistic device became a virtue only when it contributed to the effectiveness of the passage in which it occurred:

> I know that this study of sentence and paragraph length has been beneficial to me, but I would like to consider the choice and arrangement of words used by professional authors. I may be wrong, but to me an author's word choice and word arrangement is more important than the length of his sentences and paragraphs.
>
> . . . . .
>
> I believe, however, that this comparison between my prose and Lucas's reveals simply a difference in style and that no definite decisions can be made about what I should do with my prose style. In order to make such a decision, I would have to compare my vocabulary and sentence structure with Mr. Lucas's when both of us were writing on the same subject-matter.
>
> . . . . .
>
> In general, style depends on a person's individuality and his basic knowledge of English grammar. It doesn't depend on how long the sentences are or how short they are. Mr. Lucas has successfully combined English grammar with his own personal touch to produce a good piece of prose. My own style suffers from the fact that my knowledge of English grammar has not yet developed enough to aid my individuality of expression.
>
> . . . . .
>
> Although this study cannot definitely determine whether my style is good or bad (since there is no entirely good or bad style), it can show the major similarities and differences between my style and a typical modern style.
>
> . . . . .
>
> The style of a professional—in this case, F. L. Lucas—shouldn't be slavishly copied, for it is only by evolving his own style that a student gains enough command over the language to become an effective writer.
>
> . . . . .

Here are three additional charts for the tabulation of other stylistic features. Students may devise their own charts for the quantitative study of objectively observable stylistic features not included here.

Stylistic Study—II
(Grammatical Types of Sentence)

A *simple* sentence is a sentence beginning with a capital letter, containing one independent clause, and ending with terminal punctuation.

A *compound* sentence is a sentence beginning with a capital letter, containing two or more independent clauses, and ending with terminal punctuation.

A *complex* sentence is a sentence beginning with a capital letter, containing one independent clause and one or more dependent clauses, and ending with terminal punctuation.

A *compound-complex* sentence is a sentence beginning with a capital letter, containing two or more independent clauses and one or more dependent clauses, and ending with terminal punctuation.

Title of professional essay _____
Author _____

	PROFESSIONAL	STUDENT
A. Total number of sentences in essay	___	___
B. Total number of simple sentences	___	___
C. Percentage of simple sentences	___	___
D. Total number of compound sentences	___	___
E. Percentage of compound sentences	___	___
F. Total number of complex sentences	___	___
G. Percentage of complex sentences	___	___
H. Total number of compound-complex sentences		
I. Percentage of compound-complex sentences	___	___

Sequence of Grammatical Types

Set down the sequence of grammatical types in paragraphs _____ and _____, using these abbreviations: S, Cp, Cx, Cp-Cx.
In _____ paragraph: _____
In _____ paragraph: _____

Stylistic Study—III
(Sentence Openers)

Title of professional essay _____
Author _____

For this study, use only *declarative* sentences. No interrogative or imperative sentences.

Total number of declarative sentences: Professional_____   Student_____

Sentences Beginning with	Professional		Student	
	No.	%	No.	%
A. Subject (e.g., *John* broke the window. *the high cost* of living will offset . . .)	—	—	—	—
B. Expletive (e.g., *It* is plain that . . . *There* are ten Indians. Exclamations: *Alas, Oh*)	—	—	—	—

Sentences Beginning with	Professional		Student	
	No.	%	No.	%
C. Coordinating conjunction (e.g., *and, but, or nor, for, yet, so*)	—	—	—	—
D. Adverb word (e.g., *first, thus, moreover, nevertheless, namely*)	—	—	—	—
E. Conjunctive phrase (e.g., *on the other hand, as a consequence*)	—		—	
F. Prepositional phrase (e.g., *after the game, in the morning*)	—	—	—	—
G. Verbal phrase (e.g., participal, gerundive, or infinitive phrase)	—	—	—	—
H. Adjective phrase (e.g., *Tired but happy,* we . . .)	—	—	—	—
I. Absolute phrase (e.g., *The ship having arrived safely,* we . . .)	—	—	—	—
J. Adverb clause (e.g., *When the ship arrived safely,* we . . .)	—	—	—	—
K. Front-Shift (e.g., inverted word order: The expense we could not bear. Gone was the wind. Happy were they to be alive.)	—	—	—	—

Stylistic Study—IV
(Diction)

Title of professional essay
Author

For this investigation, confine yourself to this range of paragraphs: paragraph ___ through ___. For the investigation of your own prose, confine yourself to a comparable number of paragraphs.

In A, B, and C, below, count only *substantive words*—nouns, pronouns, verbs, verbals, adjectives, and adverbs.

	PROFESSIONAL	STUDENT
A. Total number of substantive words in the passage	___	___
B. Total number of monosyllabic substantive words	___	___
C. Percentage of monosyllabic substantive words	___	___
D. Total number of nouns and pronouns in the passage	___	___
E. Total number of *concrete* nouns and pronouns	___	___
F Percentage of concrete nouns and pronouns	___	___
G. Total number of *finite verbs* in all dependent and independent clauses in the passage	___	___

	PROFESSIONAL	STUDENT
H. What percentage does G represent of A?	_____	_____
I. Total number of linking verbs	_____	_____
J. Percentage of linking verbs (using A)	_____	_____
K. Total number of active verbs (do not count linking verbs)	_____	_____
L. Percentage of active verbs (using A)	_____	_____
M. Total number of passive verbs (do not count linking verbs)	_____	_____
N. Percentage pf passive verbs (using A)	_____	_____
O. Total number of adjectives in the passage (do not count participles or articles)	_____	_____
P. Average number of adjectives per sentence (divide by the total number of sentences in the passage)	_____	_____

So much for this discussion of what to look for when you analyze prose style. You will be further aided in developing your own style and in developing a technique for analyzing style by practicing some of the imitation exercises recommended in a later section of this chapter. You are also urged to read the stylistic analyses of Addison's *Spectator* essay and of President Kennedy's Inaugural Address at the end of this chapter.

Figures of Speech

We come now to a consideration of figures of speech. It is fair enough to regard figures of speech as the "graces of language," as the "dressing of thought," as "embellishments," for indeed they do "decorate" our prose and give it "style," in the courturier's sense. But it would be a mistake to regard embellishment as the chief or sole function of figures. The classical rhetoricians certainly did not look upon them as decorative devices primarily. Metaphor, according to Aristotle, did give "charm and distinction" to our expression; but even more than that, metaphor was another way to *give* "clearness" and "liveliness" to the expression of our thoughts. Figures, in his view, provided one of the best ways to strike that happy balance between "the obvious and the obscure," so that our audience could grasp our ideas promptly and thereby be disposed to accept our arguments.

"What, then, can oratorical imagery effect?" Longinus asked. He was even more explicit than Aristotle in pointing out the rhetorical function of figures: "Well, it is able in many ways to infuse vehemence and passion into spoken words, while more particularly when it is combined with the argumentative passages it not only persuades the hearer but actually makes him its slave."—*On the Sublime*, XV, 9.

It was Quintilian who most explicitly related the figures to the *logos*, *pathos*, and *ēthos* of argument. Quintilian looked upon the figures as another means of lending "credibility to our arguments," of "exciting the emotions," and of winning "approval for our characters as pleaders" (*Instit. Orat.*, IX, i). This view of the function of figures of speech is perhaps the most reliable attitude to adopt toward these devices of style. Because figures can render our thoughts vividly concrete, they help us to communicate with our audience clearly and effectively; because they stir emotional responses, they can carry truth, in Wordsworth's phrase, "alive into the heart by passion"; and because they elicit admiration for the eloquence of the speaker or writer, they can exert a powerful ethical appeal.

Sister Miriam Joseph in her book *Shakespeare's Use of the Arts of Language* reclassified the more than 200 figures distinguished by the Tudor rhetoricians according to the four categories: grammar, logos, pathos, and ethos. By classifying the figures in this way, she was able to demonstrate, quite convincingly, that the three "schools" of rhetoric during the Renaissance (the Ramists, the traditionalists, and the figurists) saw the figures as being intimately connected with the topics of invention. Metaphor, for instance, involving comparison of like things, is tied up with the topic of similarity; antithesis, involving the juxtaposition of opposites, is tied up with the topic of dissimilarity or of contraries. Then there were figures, like apostrophe, that were calculated to work directly on the emotions, and figures, like *comprobatio*, that were calculated to establish the ethical image of the speaker or writer. In our exposition, we will frequently point out the relationship of the figures either with grammar or with the three modes of persuasive appeal.

The mention of two hundred figures of speech in the previous paragraph may have appalled you. If pressed, you could name—even if you could not define or illustrate—a half dozen figures of speech. But where did those *other* figures come from? and what are they? In their passion for anatomizing and categorizing knowledge, the humanists of the Renaissance delighted in classifying and sub-classifying the figures. Admittedly, they were being overly subtle in distinguishing such a multitude of figures. The most widely used classical handbook in the Renaissance schools, *Rhetorica ad Herennium*, required the students to learn only 65 figures. Susenbrotus, in his popular *Epitome troporum ac schematum* (1540), distinguished 132 figures. But Henry Peacham, in his 1577 edition of *The Garden of Eloquence*, pushed the number up to 184. Pity the poor Tudor school children who were expected to define and illustrate and to use in their own compositions a goodly number of these figures.

We are not going to plague you with a long catalogue of figures, but we are going to introduce more figures than you have met with in your previous study of style. If nothing else, you should become aware, through this exposure, that your language has more figurative resources than you were conscious of. And you may discover that you have been using many of the figures of speech all your life. For people did not begin to use figures of speech only after academicians had classified and defined them; rather, the figures were classified and defined after people had been using them for centuries. Like the principles of grammar, poetics, and rhetoric, the doctrine of the figures was arrived at inductively. Rhetoricians merely gave "names" to the verbal practices of human beings.

What do we mean by the term "figures of speech"? We mean the same thing that Quintilian means when he used the term *figura*: "any deviation, either in thought or expression, from the ordinary and simple method of speaking, a change analogous to the different positions our bodies assume when we sit down, lie down, or look back. . . . Let the definition of a figure, therefore, be *a form of speech artfully varied from common usage* (Ergo figura sit arte aliqua novata forma dicendi)"—*Instit. Orat.*, IX, i. 11.

We will use "figures of speech" as the generic term for any artful deviations from the ordinary mode of speaking or writing. But we will divide the figures of speech into two main groups—the *schemes* and the *tropes*. A scheme (Greek *schēma*, form, shape) involves a deviation from the ordinary pattern or arrangement of words. A trope (Greek *tropein*, to turn) involves a deviation from the ordinary and principal signification of a word.

Both types of figures involves a *transference* of some kind: a trope, a transference of meaning; a scheme, a transference of order. When Shakespeare's Mark Antony said, "Brutus is an honorable man," he was using the trope called irony, because he was "transferring" the ordinary meaning of the word *honorable* to convey a different meaning to his audience. If Mark Antony had said, "Honorable is the man who gives his life for his country," he would have been using a species of the scheme hyperbaton, because he would be "transferring" the usual order of words. In a sense, of course, both schemes and tropes involve a change of "meaning," since both result in effects that are different from the ordinary mode of expression. But for all practical purposes, our distinction is clear enough to enable you to distinguish between a scheme and a trope.

The terms used to label the various figures appear formidable—strange, polysyllabic words, most of them merely transliterated from the Greek. But technical terms, in any discipline, are always difficult at first sight; they are difficult, however, mainly because they are unfamiliar. Whenever we study a new discipline we have to learn the "names" of things peculiar to that discipline. Inevitably these specialized terms will be puzzling, but they will remain puzzling only until we learn to connect the *sign* with the concept or thing for which it stands. The word *tree* is difficult for the child only until he or she learns to associate the sound or the graphic mark of this word with the thing that it designates. The term *prosopopeia* may frighten you at first, but once you get to the point where you can immediately associate the term with its significance, *prosopopeia* will be no more frightening to you than the familiar terms *metaphor* and *simile*. We could, as the Renaissance rhetorician George Puttenham tried to do, invent English terms for the various figures, but since they would have to be coined terms, they would not necessarily be any easier to learn than the classical terms. However, wherever a familiar

Angelicized term exists for a figure, we will use that term instead of the classical one.

In any case, we must not look upon terminology as an end in itself. Just as we can speak and write our native language without knowing the names of the parts of speech, so we can use and respond to figurative language without knowing the names of the figures. Nomenclature, in any study, is a convenience for purposes of classification and discussion. But an awareness of the various figures of speech can increase our verbal resources, and if we make a conscious effort to learn the figures of speech, it is likely that we will resort to them more often.

The Schemes

Schemes of Words

We shall not dwell very long on schemes of words because while they occur frequently in poetry—especially in the poetry of earlier centuries—they rarely occur in prose. The schemes of words (sometimes called *orthographical schemes*, because they involve changes in the spelling or sound of words) are formed (1) by adding or subtracting a letter or a syllable at the beginning, middle, or end of a word, or (2) by exchanging sounds. Terms like the following are of more concern to the grammarian and the prosodist than to the rhetorician:

> *prosthesis*—adding a syllable in front of word—e.g., *beloved* for *loved*
>
> *epenthesis*—adding a syllable in the middle of word—e.g., *visitating* for *visiting*
>
> *proparalepsis*—adding a syllable at the end of word—e.g., *climature* for *climate*
>
> *aphaeresis*—subtracting a syllable from the beginning of word—e.g., *'neath* for *beneath*
>
> *syncope*—subtracting a syllable from the middle of word—e.g., *prosprous* for *prosperous*
>
> *apocope*—subtracting a syllable from the end of word—e.g., *even* for *evening*
>
> *metathesis*—transposition of letters in a word—e.g., *clapse* for *clasp*
>
> *antisthecon*—change of sound—e.g., *wrang* for *wrong*

One can easily see that all of these involve a change in the shape or configuration of words. Poets used to employ such schemes to accommodate the rhyme or the rhythm of a line of verse. And because such changes are associated primarily with poetry, it is customary to regard such altered words as "poetic diction." Perhaps the situation in modern prose where we are most likely to use schemes of words would be the dialogue in a story. If a character in a story habitually clipped syllables from his words or mispronounced certain words, we might try to indicate those speech habits with spelling changes. Readers of *Finnegan's Wake* could supply numerous examples of other uses that James Joyce made of orthographical schemes in his remarkably ingenious prose.

Schemes of Construction

I. Schemes of Balance

Parallelism—similarity of structure in a pair or series of related words, phrases, or clauses.

Examples: He tried to make the law clear, precise, and equitable.

> . . . for the support of this declaration, with a firm reliance on the protection of Divine Protection, we mutually pledge to each other our Lives, our Fortunes, and our sacred Honor.—The Declaration of Independence

> We must now hope that Mr. Moynahan will devote his next decade to those four or five more novels which will banish his vacillations and uncertainties, purge his unneeded influences, and perfect his native gifts for language, landscape, and portraiture.—L. E. Sissman, *The New Yorker*

> It is certain that if you were to behold the whole woman, there is that dignity in her aspect, that composure in her motion, that complacency in her manner, that if her form makes you hope, her merit makes you fear.—Richard Steele, *Spectator*, No. 113

> I am a simple citizen who wants to live in peace and not be taxed out of existence or poisoned out of oxygen or sonically boomed out of my sanity and my home by all the things you do to help me, to defend me, to better provide me speed, electricity, national prestige, and freedom from bugs.—Talk of the Town, *The New Yorker*

> It is rather for us to be here dedicated to the great task remaining before us—that from those honored dead we take increased devotion to that cause for which they gave the last full measure of devotion; that we here highly resolve that these dead shall not have died in vain; that this nation, under God, shall have a new birth of freedom; and that government of the people, by the people, for the people, shall not perish from the earth.—Abraham Lincoln

Parallelism is one of the basic principles of grammar and rhetoric. The principle demands that equivalent things be set forth in co-ordinate grammatical structures. So nouns must be yoked with nouns, prepositional phrases with prepositional phrases, adverb clauses with adverb clauses. When this principle is ignored, not only is the grammar of co-ordination violated, but the rhetoric of coherence is wrenched. Students must be made to realize that violations of parallelism are serious, not only because they impair communication but because they reflect disorderly thinking. Whenever you see a co-ordinating conjunction in one of your sentences, you should check to make sure that the elements joined by the conjunction are of the same grammatical kind. Such a check might prevent you from writing sentences like these, all taken from student papers:

> Teenagers who dance the frug or the jerk are either wild or juvenile delinquents or both.

> Other common complaints are the failure of *Webster's Third* to include encyclopedic matter and for its technique of definition.

> Was this act rational and premeditated, or was it irrational and a spur-of-the-moment?

> He sounds like a nobleman threatened with revolution and who fears liberation of the masses.

> This situation not only is a problem for the fan, but it also affects the athletes. (A common violation of parallelism when correlative conjunctions are used.)

When the parallel elements are similar not only in structure but in length (that is, the same number of words, even the same number of syllables), the scheme is called **isocolon** (ī-sō-cō'-lon). For example: His purpose was *to impress the ignorant, to perplex the dubious*, and *to confound the scrupulous*. The addition of symmetry of length to similarity of structure contributes greatly to the rhythm of sentences. Obviously, you should not strive for isocolon every time you produce parallel structure. Such regularity of rhythm would approach the recurrent beat of verse.

Since parallelism is a device that we resort to when we are specifying or enumerating pairs or series of like things, it is easy to see the intimate relationship between this device of form and the topic of similarity. See the analysis of the rhetorical effect of parallelism in Clark Kerr's sentence in the previous section.

Antithesis (an-tith'-ə-sis)—the juxtaposition of contrasting ideas, often in parallel structure.

Examples: Though studious, he was popular; though argumentative, he was modest; though inflexible, he was candid; and though metaphysical, yet orthodox.—Dr. Samuel Johnson on the character of the Reverend Zacariah Mudge, in the *London Chronicle*, May 2, 1769

Essex thought him wanting in zeal as a friend; Elizabeth thought him wanting in duty as a subject.—Thomas Babington Macaulay, "Francis Bacon" (1837)

Our knowledge separates as well as it unites; our orders disintegrate as well as bind; our art brings us together and sets us apart.—J. Robert Oppenheimer, *The Open Mind* (1955)

Those who have been left out, we will try to bring in. Those left behind, we will help to catch up.—Richard M. Nixon, Inaugural Address, January 20, 1969

That's one small step for a man, one giant leap for mankind.—Neil Armstrong, as he stepped on the moon, Sunday, July 20, 1969

It is the best of times, yet the worst of times: we live in unparalleled prosperity, yet have starvation; modern science can perform miracles to save lives, yet we have war; we balance ourselves delicately on the moon, yet destroy the delicate balance of the earth. Young people search for meaning in life, yet are confused, demoralized, frustrated.—Jesse E. Hobson and Martin E. Robbins, from an article in *America*, December 27, 1969

By the time it's empty, life will be full.—Caption for a magazine ad picturing a bottle of Canoe, a men's cologne by Dana.

It was the unknown author of *Rhetorica ad Alexandrum* who most clearly pointed up the fact that the opposition in an *antithesis* can reside either in the words or in the ideas or in both:

> An antithesis occurs when both the wording and the sense, or one or other of them, are opposed in a contrast. The following would be an antithesis both of wording and sense: "It is not fair that my opponent should become rich by possessing what belongs to me, while I sacrifice my property and become a mere beggar." In the following sentence we have a merely verbal antithesis: "Let the rich and prosperous give to the poor and needy"; and an antithesis of sense only in the following: "I tended him when he was sick, but he has been the cause of very great misfortune to me." Here there is no verbal antithesis, but the two actions are contrasted. The double antithesis (that is, both of sense and of wording) would be the best to use; but the other two kinds are also true antitheses. (From *Rhetorica ad Alexandrum*, Ch. 26, trans. E. S. Forster.)

Nicely managed, antithesis can produce the effect of aphoristic neatness and can win for the author a reputation for wit. Antithesis is obviously related to the topic of dissimilarity and the topic of contraries. (See the analysis of antithesis in Clark Kerr's sentence.)

2. *Schemes of unusual or inverted word order* (hyperbaton)

Anastrophe (a-năs´-trō-fē)—Inversion of the natural or usual word order.

Examples: Backward run the sentences, till reels the mind. (From a parody of the style of *Time* Magazine.)

The question between preaching extempore and from a written discourse, it does not properly fall within the province of this treatise to discuss on any but what may be called rhetorical principles.—Richard Whately, *Elements of Rhetoric* (1828)

The emotional isolation, the preoccupation with God and themselves, the struggles for freedom, which seem to have possessed many of my friends at the same age, I know almost nothing of.—C. P. Snow, *The Search*

Puffed-up asses Arcangeli and Bottini unquestionably are.—Richard D. Altick and James F. Loucks, *Browning's Roman Murder Story* (1968)

I got, so far as the immediate moment was concerned, away.—Henry James, *The Turn of the Screw*

Rich, famous, proud, a ruling despot Pope might be—but he *was* middle class!—V. S. Pritchett, from a review in the *New York Review of Books*, February 27, 1969

Good musicians of their type they are. Clean and neat in appearance they are. Needed, we might say, they are.—Student paper

People that he had known all his life he didn't really know.—Student paper

One ad does not a survey make.—Caption from an ad for Peugeot automobiles

Perfectly does *anastrophe* conform to our definition of a scheme as "an artful deviation from the ordinary pattern or arrangement of words." Because such deviation surprises expectation, anastrophe can be an effective device for gaining attention. But its chief function is to secure emphasis. It is commonplace that the beginning and end of a clause are the positions of greatest emphasis. Words placed in those positions draw special attention and when those initial or terminal words are not normally found in those positions, they receive extraordinary emphasis.

Parenthesis (pə-ren'-thə-sis)—insertion of some verbal unit in a position that interrupts the normal syntactical flow of the sentence.

Examples But wherein any man is bold—I am speaking foolishly—I also am bold. . . . Are they ministers of Christ? I—to speak as a fool—am more.—St. Paul, 2 Cor. 11, 21 and 23

But when Savage was provoked, and very small offences were sufficient to provoke him, he would prosecute his revenge with the utmost acrimony till his passion had subsided.—Samuel Johnson, *Life of Richard Savage*

All that remained for the moment was to decide where I would go to graduate school, and that question was settled—the "snobs" had been right—by a Kellett Fellowship and then a Fulbright Scholarship to boot.—Norman Podhoretz, *Making It* (1967)

Any theory of post-historical society—our sense of being "in history" is largely determined by the pressure of political and social conflicts—will have to consider the dilemma of human motivations in the just city.—George Steiner, *Language and Silence* (1967)

However far the interpreters alter the text (another notorious example is the Rabbinic and Christian "spiritual" interpretations of the clearly erotic Song of Songs), they must claim to be reading off a sense that is already there.—Susan Sontag, *Against Interpretation* (1966)

He said he supervised ten editors—another euphemism—in his department, which clears 90% of NBC's entertainment programming, including movies.—Joan Barthel, from an article in *Life,* August 1, 1969

There is even, and it is the achievement of this book, a curious sense of happiness running through its paragraphs.—Norman Mailer, from a book review in *Cannibals and Christians* (1966)

The distinguishing mark of *parenthesis* is that the interpolated member is "cut off" from the syntax of the rest of the sentence. A parenthesis abruptly—and usually briefly—sends the thought off on a tangent. Although the parenthetical matter is not necessary for the grammatical completeness of the sentence, it does have a pronounced rhetorical effect. For a brief moment, we hear the author's voice, commenting, editorializing, and, for that reason, the sentence gets an emotional charge that it would otherwise not have. Note, for instance, the difference in effect if the parenthetical element in St. Paul's first sentence is syntactically integrated with the rest of the sentence: "But I am speaking foolishly if I claim that wherein any man is bold, I also am bold."

Apposition (ap-ə-zish′-en)—placing side by side two co-ordinate elements, the second of which serves as an explanation or modification of the first.

Examples: John Morgan, the president of the Sons of the Republic, could not be reached by phone.

Men of this kind—soldiers of fortune, pool-hall habitués, gigolos, beachcombers—expend their talents on trivialities.—Student paper

Apart from the association of Latin with rhetoric as an art, this last mentioned fact, that Latin was totally controlled by writing no matter how much it was used for speech, produced other special kinds of drives toward the oral within the academic world.—Walter J. Ong, from an article in *PMLA*, June 1965

So we would have gone together, the Orthodox and I.—George Steiner, from an article in *Commentary*, February 1965

A miscellaneous list, this, but all of the items on it are characterized by the same misunderstandings and misconceptions of the nature of American power; and all have this in common, that they defy solution so long as the energies and resources of the nation are monopolized by the war in Vietnam.—Henry Steele Commager, from a book review in the *New York Review of Books*, December 5, 1968

Apposition is such a common method of expansion in modern prose that it hardly seems to conform to our definition of a scheme as "an artful deviation from the ordinary patterns of speech." But if we reflect upon our own experience, we will have to acknowledge that appositional structures seldom occur in impromptu speech. Apposition may not be the exclusive property of written prose, but it certainly occurs most frequently in written prose—in a situation, in other words, where we have time to make a conscious choice of our arrangement of words. So there is something *artful* about the use of the appositive. And there is something out-of-the-ordinary about the appositive, too. Although the appositive does not disturb the natural flow of the sentence as violently as parenthetical expressions do (mainly because the appositive is grammatically co-ordinate with the unit that it follows), it does interrupt the flow of the sentence, interrupts the flow to supply some gratuitous information or explanation.

3. Schemes of Omission

Ellipsis (ĕ-lip′-sis)—deliberate omission of a word or of words which are readily implied by the context.

Examples: And he to England shall along with you.—*Hamlet*, III, iii, 4

Kant, we may suppose, was more startled by Hume's apparent destruction of all basis for philosophical certainty; Reid, by the remoter consequences to morality and theology.—Sir Leslie Stephen, *History of English Thought in the Eighteenth Century* (1876)

So singularly clear was the water that when it was only twenty or thirty feet deep the bottom seemed floating in the air! Yes, where it was even *eighty* feet deep. Every little pebble was distinct, every speckled trout, every hand's-breadth of sand.—Mark Twain, *Roughing It*

As with religion, so with education. In colonial New England, education was broad-based, but nevertheless elitist; and in its basic assumptions, intellectualist.—David Marquand, from an article in *Encounter*, March 1964

Rape is the sexual sin of the mob, adultery of the bourgeoisie, and incest of the aristocracy.—John Updike, from a book review in the *New Yorker*, August 2, 1969

So let the class invent its own assignments. If it wants more sophistication, fine.—Peter Elbow, from an article in *College English*, November 1968

The Master's degree is awarded by seventy-four departments, and the Ph.D. by sixty.—Student paper

Ellipsis can be an artful and arresting means of securing economy of expression. We must see to it, however, that the understood words are grammatically compatible. If we wrote, "The ringleader was hanged, and his accomplices imprisoned," we would be guilty of a solecism, because the understood *was* is not grammatically compatible with the plural subject (*accomplices*) of the second clause. And we produce a "howler" if we say, "While in the fourth grade, my father took me to the zoo."

Asyndeton (a-sin´-də-ton)—deliberate omission of conjunctions between a series of related clauses.

Examples: I came, I saw, I conquered.

They may have it in well-doing, they may have it in learning, they may have it even in criticism.—Matthew Arnold

The infantry plodded forward, the tanks rattled into position, the big guns swung their snouts toward the rim of the hills, the planes raked the underbrush with gunfire.

The Tudor rhetoricians had a special name for the omission of conjunctions between single words or phrases. They would have labelled the following as instances of **brachylogia** (brak-ə-lo´-jē-a):

. . . and that government of the people, by the people, for the people, shall not perish from the earth.—Abraham Lincoln

. . . that we shall pay any price, bear any burden, meet any hardship, support any friend, oppose any foe to assure the survival and the success of liberty.—John F. Kennedy

But there seems to be no good reason why we cannot use the single term *asyndeton* for all these instances of omission of conjunctions. The principal effect of asyndeton is to produce a hurried rhythm in the sentence. Aristotle observed that asyndeton was especially appropriate for the conclusion of a discourse, because there, perhaps more than in other places in the discourse, we may want to produce the emotional reaction that can be stirred by, among other means, rhythm. And Aristotle concluded his *Rhetoric* with an instance of asyndeton that is noticeable even in translation: "I have done. You have heard me. The facts are before you. I ask for your judgment."

The opposite scheme is **polysyndeton** (pol-ē-sin′-də-ton) (deliberate use of many conjunctions). Note how the proliferation of conjunctions in the following quotation slows up the rhythm of the prose and produces an impressively solemn note:

> And God said, "Let the earth bring forth living creatures according to their kinds: cattle and creeping things and beasts of the earth according to their kinds." And it was so. And God made the beasts of the earth according to their kinds and the cattle according to their kinds and everything that creeps upon the ground according to its kind. And God saw that it was good.—Genesis, 1:24–25

Ernest Hemingway uses polysyndeton to create another effect. Note how the repeated *and*'s in the following passage suggest the flow and continuity of experience:

> I said, "Who killed him?" and he said, "I don't know who killed him but he's dead all right," and it was dark and there was water standing in the street and no lights and windows broke and boats all up in the town and trees blown down and everything all blown and I got a skiff and went out and found my boat where I had her inside Mango Key and she was all right only she was full of water.—Hemingway, "After the Storm"

Polysyndeton can be used to produce special emphasis. Note the difference in effect of these two sentences:

> This semester I am taking English, history, biology, mathematics, sociology, and physical education.

> This semester I am taking English and history and biology and mathematics and sociology and physical education.

4. Schemes of Repetition

Alliteration (ə-lit-er-ā′-shən)—repetition of initial or medial consonants in two or more adjacent words.

Examples: A sable, silent, solemn forest stood.
                              —James Thomson, "The Castle of Indolence," 1. 38

> Progress is not proclamation nor palaver. It is not pretense nor play on prejudice. It is not the perturbation of a people passion-wrought nor a promise proposed.—Warren G. Harding nominating William Howard Taft in 1912

Already American vessels had been searched, seized, and sunk.
>—John F. Kennedy, *Profiles in Courage*

A moist young moon hung above the mist of a neighboring meadow.—Vladimir Nabokov, *Conclusive Evidence*

I should hear him fly with the high fields
And wake to the farm forever fled from the childless land.
>—Dylan Thomas, "Fern Hill," ll. 50–51

Tart, tingling, and even ticklish.—Caption from an ad for Sprite

We double-distill a dram at a time, instead of taking the faster big batch away.—Caption from an ad for Old Grand-Dad bourbon

In Anglo-Saxon poetry, *alliteration* rather than rhyme was the device to bind verses together. Because it contributes to the euphony of verse or prose, alliteration became a conspicuous feature of Euphuistic prose and Romantic poetry. Because it is such an obvious mannerism, alliteration is rarely used in modern prose. It is sometimes used today, however, for special effects—as a mnemonic device for slogans (Better Business Builds Bigger Bankrolls) and advertising catch-lines (Spark*l*ing . . . *Fl*avorful . . . Mi*ll*er High Life . . . The Champagne of Bott*l* Beer . . . *Br*ewed on*ly* in Mi*l*waukee.) Sometimes alliteration is deliberately used for humorous effect: He was a preposterously pompous proponent of precious pedantry.

Assonance (as'-ə-nəns)—the repetition of similar vowel sounds, preceded and followed by different consonants, in the stressed syllables of adjacent words.

Examples: An old, mad, bl*i*nd, desp*i*sed, and dying king—
Pr*i*nces, the dregs of their d*u*ll race, who flow
Through p*u*blic scorn—m*u*d from a m*u*ddy spring—
>—Shelley, "Sonnet: England in 1819"

Had Gray written often thus, it had been v*ai*n to bl*a*me and useless to pr*ai*se him.—Samuel Johnson, *Life of Thomas Gray*

Under a juniper-tree the bones s*a*ng, sc*a*ttered and shining We were glad to be sc*a*ttered, we did little good to each other Under a tree in the cool of the day, with the shining s*a*nd—T. S. Elliot, "Ash Wednesday"

Wh*a*les in the w*a*ke like c*a*pes and Alps
Qu*a*ked the sick sea and snouted deep
>—Dylan Thomas, "Ballad of the Long-Legged Bait"

Refr*e*sh your z*e*st for living
>—Caption from an ad for French Line Ships

Assonance, a device of sound, like alliteration, is used mainly in poetry. A prose writer might deliberately use assonance to produce certain onomato-poetic or humorous effects. The danger for the prose writer, however, lies in the careless repetition of similar vowel-sounds, producing awkward jingles like this: "He tries to revise the evidence supplied by his eyes."

Anaphora (ə-naf'-ə-rə)—repetition of the same word or group of words at the beginnings of successive clauses.

Examples: The Lord sitteth above the water floods. The Lord remaineth a King forever. The Lord shall give strength unto his people. The Lord shall give his people the blessing of peace.—Psalm 29

We shall fight on the beaches, we shall fight on the landing-grounds, we shall fight in the fields and in the streets, we shall fight in the hills.—Winston Churchill, speech in the House of Commons, June 4, 1940

We are moving to the land of freedom. Let us march to the realization of the American dream. Let us march on segregated housing. Let us march on segregated schools. Let us march on poverty. Let us march on ballot boxes, march on ballot boxes until race baiters disappear from the political arena, until the Wallaces of our nation tremble away in silence.—Martin Luther King, Jr., on a civil-rights march from Selma to Montgomery, Alabama, 1965

They are common just as theft, cheating, perjury, adultery have always been common. They were common, not because people did not know what was right, but because people liked to do what was wrong. They were common, though prohibited by law. They were common, though condemned by public opinion. They were common, because in that age law and public opinion united had not sufficient force to restrain the greediness of powerful and unprincipled magistrates.—Thomas Babington Macaulay, "Francis Bacon," 1837

Why should white people be running all the stores in our community? Why should white people be running the banks of our community? Why should the economy of our community be in the hands of the white man? Why?—Speech by Malcolm X

It is a luxury, it is a privilege, it is an indulgence for those who are at their ease.—Edmund Burke, "Letter to a Noble Lord," 1796

It is 1969 already, and 1965 seems almost like a childhood memory. Then we were the conquerors of the world. No one could stop us. We were going to end the war. We were going to wipe out racism. We were going to mobilize the poor. We were going to take over the universities.—Jerry Rubin, from an article in the *New York Review of Books*, February 13, 1969

Whenever anaphora occurs, we can be sure that the author has used it deliberately. Since the repetition of the words helps to establish a marked rhythm in the sequence of clauses, this scheme is usually reserved for those passages where the author wants to produce a strong emotional effect. Note how Reinhold Niebuhr combines anaphora with plays on words to produce this neat aphorism: "Man's capacity for justice makes democracy possible; but man's inclination to injustice makes democracy necessary."

Epistrophe (ə-pis'-trō-fē)—repetition of the same word or group of words at the ends of successive clauses.

Examples: Shylock: I'll have my bond! Speak not against my bond!
              I have sworn an oath that I will have my bond!
                                   —*The Merchant of Venice*, III, iii, 3–4

> To the good American many subjects are sacred: sex is sacred, women are sacred, children are sacred, business is sacred, America is sacred, Mason lodges and college clubs are sacred.—George Santayana, *Character and Opinion in the United States*

> But to all those who would be tempted by weakness, let us leave no doubt that we will be as strong as we need to be for as long as we need to be.

> . . . We cannot learn from one another until we stop shouting at one another.—Richard M. Nixon, Inaugural Address, January 20, 1969

> Perhaps this is the most important thing for me to take back from beach-living: simply the memory that each cycle of the tide is valid, each cycle of the wave is valid, each cycle of a relationship is valid. —Anne Lindbergh, *Gift from the Sea*

> As long as the white man sent you to Korea, you bled. He sent you to Germany, you bled. He sent you to the South Pacific to fight the Japanese, you bled.—Speech by Malcolm X

> In a cake, nothing tastes like real butter, nothing moistens like real butter, nothing enriches like real butter, nothing satisfies like real butter.—Caption from a Pillsbury ad

> He's learning fast. Are you earning fast?—Caption from an ad for Aetna Life Insurance

Epistrophe not only sets up a pronounced rhythm but secures a special emphasis, both by repeating the word and by putting the word in the final position in the sentence.

Epanalepsis (ə-pon-ə-lep′-sis)—repetition at the end of a clause of the word that occurred at the beginning of the clause.

Examples: Blood hath bought blood, and blows have answer'd blows:
Strength match'd with strength, and power confronted power.
—Shakespeare, *King John*, II, i, 329–30

Year chases year, decay pursues decay.—Samuel Johnson, "The Vanity of Human Wishes"

Possessing what we still were unpossessed by,
Possessed by what we now no more possessed.
—Robert Frost, "The Gift Outright"

And when the shadow fades and is no more, the light that lingers becomes a shadow to another light.—Kahlil Gibran, *The Prophet*

A nut nut is a person who is nuts about the fun of eating nuts.
—Caption from an ad for Skippy Peanut Butter

Business forms are as various as people forms.—Caption from an ad for Nekoosa Paper Company

Epanalepsis is rare in prose, probably because when the emotional situation arises that can make such a scheme appropriate, poetry seems to be the only form that can adequately express the emotion. It would seem perfectly natural for a father to express his grief over the death of a beloved son in this fashion: "He was flesh of my flesh, bone of my bone, blood of my blood." But would the father be speaking prose or poetry? Perhaps the only answer we could give is that it is heightened language of some sort, the kind of language which, despite its appearance of contrivance, springs spontaneously from intense emotion. Repetition, we know, is one of the characteristics of highly emotional language. And in this instance what better way for the father to express the intimacy of the relationship with his son than by the repetition of words at the beginning and end of successive groups of words?

Perhaps the best general advice about the use of epanalepsis—in fact of all those schemes that are appropriate only to extraordinary circumstances— would be, "If you find yourself consciously deciding to use epanalepsis, don't use it." When the time is appropriate, the scheme will present itself unbidden.

Anadiplosis (an-ə-di-plō′-sis)—repetition of the last word of one clause at the beginning of the following clause.

Examples: Labor and care are rewarded with success, success produces confidence, confidence relaxes industry, and negligence ruins the reputation which diligence had raised.—Dr. Johnson, *Rambler* No. 21

They point out what is perfectly obvious, yet seldom realized: That if you have a lot of things you cannot move about a lot, that furniture requires dusting, dusters require servants, servants require insurance stamps. . . . It [property] produces men of weight. Men of weight cannot, by definition, move like the lightning from the East unto the West.—E. M. Forster, "My Wood," *Abinger Harvest*

The crime was common, common be the pain.—Alexander Pope, "Eloisa to Abelard"

The laughter had to be gross or it would turn to sobs, and to sob would be to realize, and to realize would be to despair.—John Howard Griffin, *Black Like Me*

Having power makes it [totalitarian leadership] isolated; isolation breeds insecurity; insecurity breeds suspicion and fear; suspicion and fear breed violence.—Zbigniew K. Brzezinski, *The Permanent Purge, Politics in Soviet Totalitarianism*

Queeg: "Aboard my ship, excellent performance is standard. Standard performance is sub-standard. Sub-standard performance is not permitted to exist."—Herman Wouk, *The Caine Mutiny*

Climax (klī´-maks)—arrangement of words, phrases, or clauses in an order of increasing importance.

Examples: More than that, we rejoice in our sufferings, knowing that suffering produces endurance, endurance produces character, and character produces hope, and hope does not disappoint us, because God's love has been poured into our hearts through the Holy Spirit which has been given to us.—St. Paul, Romans, 5, 3–5

Let a man acknowledge obligations to his family, his country, and his God.—Student paper

Renounce my love, my life, myself—and you.—Alexander Pope, "Eloisa to Abelard"

I think we've reached a point of great decision, not just for our nation, not only for all humanity, but for life upon the earth.—George Wald, "A Generation in Search of a Future," speech delivered at MIT on March 4, 1969

When a boy lays aside his tops, his marbles, and his bike in favor of a girl, another girl, and still another girl, he becomes a youth. When the youth discards his first girl and his second girl for *the* girl, he becomes a bachelor. And when the bachelor can stand it no longer, he turns into a husband.—Alan Beck, from an article in *Good Housekeeping*, July 1957

It shreds the nerves, it vivisects the psyche—and it may even scare the living daylights out of more than a few playgoers.—A review in *Time*, January 7, 1966

Climax can be considered a scheme of repetition only when, as in the first example quoted above, it is a continued *anadiplosis* involving three or more members. Otherwise, as in the second and third examples, it is simply a scheme which arranges a series in an order of gradually rising importance. This latter variety of climax can be looked upon as a scheme related to the topic of degree, and it is the kind of climax that you will most often find in modern prose and that you will probably find occasion to use in your own prose.

Antimetabole (an-tē-mə-tab′-ō-lē)—repetition of words, in successive clauses, in reverse grammatical order.

Examples: One should eat to live, not live to eat.—Molière, *L'Avare*

> It ought to be the first endeavor of a writer to distinguish nature from custom, or that which is established because it is right from that which is right only because it is established.—Samuel Johnson, *Rambler* # 156

> This man [Lord Chesterfield] I thought had been a lord among wits; but, I find, he is only a wit among lords.—Samuel Johnson, as quoted in Boswell's *Life of Johnson*

> Mankind must put an end to war—or war will put an end to mankind.—John F. Kennedy, United Nations Speech, 1961

> Ask not what your country can do for you; ask what you can do for your country.—John F. Kennedy, Inaugural Address, 1961

> The Negro needs the white man to free him from his fears. The white man needs the Negro to free him from his guilt.—Martin Luther King, Jr., from a speech delivered in 1966

> You can take Salem out of the country, But you can't take the country out of Salem.—Caption from a Salem cigarette ad

> You like it, it likes you.—Advertising slogan for Seven-Up

All of these examples have the air of the "neatly turned phrase"—the kind of phrasing that figures in most memorable aphorisms. Would the sentence from President Kennedy's Inaugural Address be so often quoted if it had read something like this: "Do not ask what American can do for you. You would do better to ask whether your country stands in need of *your* services"? The "magic" has now gone out of the appeal. It would be a profitable exercise for the student to take several of the schemes presented in this section and convert them into ordinary prose. Such an exercise would undoubtedly reveal what the schemes add to the expression of the thought.

Chiasmus (kī-əz′-mus) ("the criss-cross")—reversal of grammatical structures in successive phrases or clauses.

Examples: By day the frolic, and the dance by night.—Samuel Johnson, "The Vanity of Human Wishes"

His time a moment, and a point his space.—Alexander Pope, *Essay on Man*, Epistle I

Exalts his enemies, his friends destroys.—John Dryden, "Absalom and Achitophe!"

It is hard to make money, but to spend it is easy.—Student paper

Language changes. So should your dictionary.—Caption from ad for *Webster's Seventh New Collegiate Dictionary*

Chiasmus is similar to *antimetabole* in that it too involves a reversal of grammatical structures in successive phrases or clauses, but it is unlike *antimetabole* in that it does not involve a repetition of words. Both *chiasmus* and *antimetabole* can be used to reinforce *antithesis*.

Polyptoton (pō-lip'-tə-tahn)—repetition of words derived from the same root.

Examples: The Greeks are *strong*, and *skilful* to their *strength*.
        Fierce to their *skill*, and to their *fierceness* valiant;
        —Shakespeare, *Troilus and Cressida*, I, i, 7–8

But alas . . . the gate is narrow, the threshold high, few are *chosen* because few *choose* to be *chosen*.—Aldous Huxley, from *Collected Essays* (1955)

Let me assert my firm belief that the only thing we have to *fear* is *fear* itself.—Franklin Delano Roosevelt, First Inaugural Address, March 1933

But in this desert country they may see the land being rendered *useless* by *overuse*.—Joseph Wood Krutch, *The Voice of the Desert* (1955)

We would like to *contain* the *uncontainable* figure in a glass.—Loren Eiseley, from an article in *Harper's*, March 1964

Not as a call to *battle*, though *embattled* we are.—John F. Kennedy, Inaugural Address

Their *blood bleeds* the nation of its sanguine assurance.—Student paper

Please, Please Me.—Title of a Beatles' song

Polyptoton is very much akin to those plays on words that we will investigate in the next section on tropes.

The Tropes

Metaphor and Simile

Metaphor (met'-ə-for)—an implied comparison between two things of unlike nature that yet have something in common.

Simile (sim'-ə-lē)—an explicit comparison between two things of unlike nature that yet have something in common.

Examples (all from student themes):

> He had a posture like a question-mark. (simile)

> On the final examination, several students went down in flames. (metaphor)

> Like an arrow, the prosecutor went directly to the point. (simile)

> The question of federal aid to parochial schools is a bramble patch. (metaphor)

> Silence settled down over the audience like a block of granite. (simile)

> Birmingham lighted a runaway fuse, and as fast as the headlines could record them, demonstrations exploded all over the country. (metaphor)

We will treat metaphor and simile together because they are so much alike. The difference between metaphor and simile lies mainly in the manner of expressing the comparison. Whereas metaphor says, "David was a lion in battle," simile says, "David was *like* a lion in battle." Both of these tropes are related to the topic of similarity, for although the comparison is made between two things of unlike nature (*David* and *lion*), there is some respect in which they are similar (e.g., they are courageous, or they fight ferociously, or they are unconquerable in a fight). The thing with which the first thing is compared is to be understood in some "transferred sense": *David* is not literally a *lion*, but he is a lion in some "other sense."

An extended or continued metaphor is known as an *allegory*. We see one of these sustained metaphors in *The Battle of the Books*, where Jonathan Swift compares the classical writers, not to the spider, which spins its web out of its own entrails, but to the far-ranging bee:

> As for us the ancients, we are content with the bee to pretend to nothing of our own, beyond our wings and our voices, that is to say, our flights and our language. For the rest, whatever we have got has been by infinite labor and search, and ranging through every corner of nature; the difference is that instead of dirt and poison, we have chosen to fill our hives with honey and wax, thus furnishing mankind with the two noblest of things, which are sweetness and light.

Closely allied to this form of extended metaphor is *parable*, an anecdotal narrative designed to teach a moral lesson. The most famous examples of parable are those found in the New Testament. In the parable of the sower of seeds, for instance, our interest is not so much in the tale of a man who went out to sow some seeds as in what each detail of the anecdote "stands for," in what the details "mean." Whenever the disciplines were puzzled about what a particular parable meant, they asked Christ to interpret it for them.

And while we are talking about these analogical tropes, we should warn writers to be on their guard against the "mixed metaphor," which results when they lose sight of the terms of their comparisons. When Joseph Addison said, "There is not a single view of human nature which is not sufficient to extinguish the seeds of pride," it is obvious that he is mixing two different metaphors. We could say "to extinguish the *flames* of pride" or "to *water* the seeds of pride," but we cannot mix the notion of extinguishing with that of seeds. The rhetoricians sometimes called such "wrenching of words" **catachresis** (kat-ə-krē′-sis).

Synecdoche (si-nek′-də-kē)—a figure of speech in which a part stands for the whole.

Examples:

> genus substituted for the species:
> *vessel* for *ship*, *weapon* for *sword*, *creature* for *man*, *arms* for *rifles*, *vehicle* for *bicycle*

> species substituted for the genus:
> *bread* for *food*, *cutthroat* for *assassin*

> part substituted for the whole:
> *sail* for *ship*, *hands* for *helpers*, *roofs* for *houses*

> matter for what is made from it:
> *silver* for *money*, *canvas* for *sail*, *steel* for *sword*

In general, we have an instance of *synecdoche* when the part or genus or adjunct that is mentioned suggests something else. It is an *oblique* manner of speaking. All of the following illustrate this trope: "Give us this day our daily *bread*." "All *hands* were summoned to the quarter-deck." "Not *marble*, nor the gilded monuments of princes, shall outlive the powerful *rhyme*." "They braved the *waves* to protect their fatherland." "Brandish your *steel*, men." "Are there no *roofs* in this town that will harbor an honorable man?" "It is pleasing to contemplate a *manufacture* rising gradually from its first mean state by the successive *labors* of innumerable *minds*."—Johnson, *Rambler* No. 9. "The door closed upon the extempore surgeon and midwife, and *Roaring Camp* sat down outside, smoked its pipe, and awaited the issue."—Bret Harte, "The Luck of Roaring Camp."

Metonymy (mə-tahn'-ə-mē)—substitution of some attributive or suggestive word for what is actually meant.

Examples: *crown* for *royalty*, *mitre* for *bishop*, *wealth* for *rich people*, *brass* for *military officers*, *bottle* for *wine*, *pen* for *writers*

Metonymy and synecdoche are so close to being the same trope that George Campbell, the eighteenth-century rhetorician, wondered whether we should make any great effort to distinguish them. Those rhetoricians who did make the effort to discriminate these tropes would label the following as examples of metonymy:

> If the nearness of our last necessity brought a nearer conformity into it, there were happiness in *haory hairs* and no calamity in *half senses*. . . . and Charles the Fifth can never hope to live within two *Methuselahs* of Hector.—Sir Thomas Browne, *Urn-Burial* (1658)

> I have nothing to offer but *blood, soil, tears*, and *sweat*.—Sir Winston Churchill, speech in the House of Commons May 13, 1940

> . . . and with firm confidence in justice, freedom, and peace on earth that will raise the hearts and the hopes of mankind for that distant day when no one *rattles a saber* and no one *drags a chain*.— Adlai Stevenson, acceptance speech, July 21, 1952

> In Europe, we gave the *cold shoulder* to De Gaulle, and now he gives the *warm hand* to Mao Tse-tung.—Richard M. Nixon, campaign speech, 1960

> You can't read the history of the United States, my friends, without learning the great story of those thousands of unnamed women. And if it's ever told straight, you'll know it's the *sunbonnet* and not the *sombrero* that has settled the country.—Edna Ferber, *Cimarron* (1930)

> *Capital* has learned to sit down and talk with *labor*.—George Meany, speech in 1966

> Breaching the *White Wall* of Southern Justice.—Title of article in *Time*, April 15, 1966

> In another song written by [Bob] Dylan and sung by the Turtles, he lectures *clinging vines* who only want a *strong shoulder* to lean on.— Review in *Time*, September 17, 1966

Puns—generic name for those figures which make a play on words.
> (1) **Antanaclasis** (an-ta-nak'-la-sis)—repetition of a word in two different senses.

>> But lest I should be condemned of introducing *license*, when I oppose *licensing*, . . . —John Milton, *Areopagitica* (1644)

If we don't *hang* together, we'll *hang* separately.—Benjamin Franklin

Your argument is *sound*, nothing but *sound*.—Benjamin Franklin

Although we're *apart*, you're still *a part* of me.—Lyrics of the song "On Blueberry Hill"

Nothing is closer to the supreme *commonplace* of our *commonplace* age than its preoccupation with *Nothing*.—Robert Martin Adams, *Nil* (1966)

You may not find this *Scotch* as smooth as Barrymore, of course, but then Barrymore wasn't *Scotch*.—Ad for Seagram's Scotch Whiskey

The *long* cigarette that's *long* on flavor.—Ad for Pall Mall cigarettes

We make the traveler's *lot* a *lot* easier.—Ad for Overseas National Airways

(2) **Paronomasia** (par-ə-nō-mā'-zha)—use of words alike in sound but different in meaning.

Neither hide nor hair of him had been seen since the day that Kwame Nkrumah had been *ostrichized*, accused of being the biggest *cheetah* in Ghana, but *safaris* anyone knew, no *fowl* play was involved.—Article in *Time*, April 8, 1966

The *Bustle*: A *Deceitful Seatful*.—Vladimir Nabokov, *Lolita*

Casting my *perils* before *swains*.—Marshall McLuhan

Fran [Elizabeth Taylor] is a chorine waiting for her paramour to obtain a divorce and *alter* her situation.—Movie review in *Time*, March 9, 1970

The end of the *plain plane, explained*.—Ad for Braniff International

One's metaphoric *retch* exceeds one's metaphoric *gasp*.—John Leonard, column in *Esquire*, February 1969

Independence is what a boy feels when all he wants from father is to be left *a loan*.—Minneapolis *Star*, April 26, 1966

The "in" idea in business travel—Hilton Inns.—Add for Hilton Inns

(3) **Syllepsis** (si-lep'-sis)—use of a word understood differently in relation to two or more other words, which it modifies or governs.

Here thou, great Anna! whom three realms obey
Dost sometimes counsel *take*—and sometimes tea.
—Alexander Pope, *The Rape of the Lock*

The play is armed with irascible wit, and Nicol Williamson's whiplash acting *raises* laughs as well as welts.—Review in *Time*, April 1, 1966

There is a certain type of woman who'd rather *press* grapes than clothes.—Ad for Peck & Peck suits

Lights are as likely to *attract* a Viet Cong bullet as a mosquito.—Article in *Time*, September 10, 1966

Who was the first to *wrap up* a case: Scotland Yard or Alexander Gordon?—Ad for Gordon's Whiskey

The ink, like our pig, keeps *running* out of the pen.—Student paper

The figure of *zeugma* (zōōg′-mə) is somewhat like syllepsis, but whereas in *syllepsis* the single word is grammatically and idiomatically compatible with both of the other words that it governs, in a *zeugma* the single word does not fit grammatically or idiomatically with one member of the pair. If we say, "Jane *has murdered* her father, and may you too" or "He maintained a *flourishing* business and racehorse," we would be producing an instance of *zeugma*, because in both sentences the *italicized* word is either grammatically or idiomatically incongruous with one member (in these examples, the second member) of the pair it governs. Those two lines from Pope's *Rape of the Lock* that are often classified as *zeugma*—"Or stain her honour, or her new brocade" and "Or lose her heart, or necklace, at a ball"—would, according to our definition, be examples of *syllepsis*. Syllepsis is the only one of these two figures that can be considered a form of pun. *Zeugma*, if skillfully managed, could be impressive as a display of wit, but often enough, *zeugma* is nothing more than a faulty use of the scheme of *ellipsis*.

Anthimeria (an-thə-mer′-ē-a)—the substitution of one part of speech for another.

Examples: I'll *unhair* thy head.—Shakespeare, *Antony and Cleopatra* II, v, 64

A mile before his tent fall down, and *knee*
The way into his mercy.—Shakespeare, *Coriolanus*, V, i, 5

The thunder would not *peace* at my bidding.—Shakespeare, *King Lear*, IV, vi, 103

That ghastly thought would drink up all your joy,
And quite *unparadise* the realms of light.
—Edward Young, *Complaint*, or *Night Thoughts*

George Rogers Clark may have camped under that tree; buffalo may have *nooned* in its shade, switching flies.—Aldo Leopold, *A Sand County Almanac* (1949)

They whack-whacked the white horse on the legs and he *kneed* himself up.—Ernest Hemingway, *in our time*

Me, *dictionary-ing* heavily, "Where was the one they were watching?"—Ernest Hemingway, *Green Hills of Africa*

Gift him with *Playboy*.—Promotional letter for *Playboy* magazine

Dozens of other examples of anthimeria could be quoted from Shakespeare's plays. If a word was not available for what he wanted to express, Shakespeare either coined a word or used an old word in a new way. Writers today must use *anthimeria* seldom and with great discretion unless they are truly masters of the existing English language. On the other hand, an apt creation can be pungent, evocative, witty, or memorable. English today is a rich, flexible language, because words have been borrowed, changed, and created. Think of all the ways in which a word like *smoke* has been used since it first came into the language:

> The smoke rose from the chimney.
> The chimney smokes.
> He smoked the ham.
> He smokes.
> She asked for a smoke.
> He objected to the smoke nuisance.
> She noticed the smoky atmosphere.
> He tried smoking on the sly.
> She smoked out the thief.
> His dreams went up in smoke.
> The Ferrari smoked along the wet track.

Someday someone will say, if it hasn't been said already, "He looked at her smokily."

Periphrasis (pǝ-rif'-ǝ-sis)—substitution of a descriptive word or phrase for a proper name or of a proper name for a quality associated with the name.

Examples The *Splendid Splinter* hit two more *round-trippers* today.

> In his later years he became in fact the most scarifying of his own creatures: a *Quixote* of the Cotswolds who abdicated his century and thereafter lived in quasi-medieval delusions that degenerated at last into melancholia.—Article on Evelyn Waugh in *Time*, April 22, 1966

> They do not escape *Jim Crow*; they merely encounter another, not less deadly variety.—James Baldwin, *Nobody Knows My Name*

> Disney's *Pollyanna* is looking more like an aging *Lolita* now, but it's perfectly all right.—Article in *Time*, April 1, 1966

> Pale young men with larded and *Valentino-black* side whiskers.— Dylan Thomas, "Memoirs of an August Bank Holiday"

> When you're out of *Schlitz*, you're out of beer.—Advertising slogan for Schlitz beer

> She may not have been a *Penelope*, but she was not as unfaithful as the gossips made her out to be.—Student paper

The frequency with which we meet this trope, even in modern prose, is evidence of the urge in man to express familiar ideas in uncommon ways. Circumlocutions and tags can become tiresome clichés (as they often do on the sports page), but when they display a fresh, decorous inventiveness, they can add grace to our writing. It is the trite or overly ingenious oblique expression that wearies the reader.

Personification or **Prosopopoeia** (prə-sō-pō-pe´-ə)—investing abstractions or inanimate objects with human qualities or abilities.

Examples: The ground thirsts for rain.—Student paper

> He glanced at the dew-covered grass, and it winked back at him.—Student paper

> A tree whose hungry mouth is prest
> Against the earth's sweet-flowing breast.
> > —Joyce Kilmer, "Trees"

> And indeed there will be time
> For the yellow smoke that slides along the street,
> Rubbing its back upon the window panes.
>   T. S. Eliot, "The Love Song of J. Alfred Prufrock"
> > —T. S. Eliot, "The Love Song of J. Alfred Prufock"

> Mother Tongue is a self-reliant female.—Charlton Laird, *The Miracle of Language*

> The handsome houses on the street to the college were not fully awake, but they looked very friendly.—Lionel Trilling, "Of This Time, Of That Place"

Personification is such a familiar figure that there is no need to multiply examples of it. This is one of the figures that should be reserved for passages designed to stir the emotions. Another emotional figure, closely allied to personification, is *apostrophe* (ə-pos´-trə-fē) (addressing an absent person or a personified abstraction). Here is an example of *apostrophe* from Sir Walter Raleigh's *History of the World*:

> O eloquent, just, and mighty Death! whom none could advise, thou hast persuaded; what none hath dared, thou hast done; and whom all the world has flattered, thou only hast cast out the world and despised. Thou hast drawn together all the far-stretched greatness, all the pride, cruelty, and ambition of man, and covered it all with these two narrow words, *Hic jacet*.

Hyperbole (hī-pur'-bə-lē)—the use of exaggerated terms for the purpose of emphasis or heightened effect.

Examples: His eloquence would split rocks.

> It's really ironical . . . I have gray hair. I really do. The one side of my head—the right side—is full of millions of gray hairs.—Holden Caulfield in *Catcher in the Rye*

> My left leg weighs three tons. It is embalmed in spices like a mummy. I can't move. I haven't moved for five thousand years. I'm of the time of Pharoah.—Thomas Bailey Aldrich, "Marjorie Daw"

> "Rozelle's right," pitched in the only man in New York still wearing a 1951 crew cut.—Rex Reed, article in *Esquire*, October 1969

> What he does not like is the press, which he tells us misrepresents him ninety percent of the time, by which we must understand, in a world of hyperbole which so naturally accentuates in a world of sport (how excruciating it must be for the sportswriter who cannot report that Joe Namath ran two hundred yards for a touchdown!) that occasionally we have got him wrong.—William F. Buckley, Jr., article in *Esquire*, October 1969

> I will buy anything—ANYTHING—that has been reduced to one third its original price.—Jean Kerr, *The Snake Has All the Lines*

> We walked along a road in Cumberland and stooped, because the sky hung so low.—Thomas Wolfe, *Look Homeward, Angel*

Hyperbole is so steadily droned into our ears that most of us have ceased to think of it as a figure of speech. Advertisers and teenagers can hardly talk without using superlatives. Perhaps we would not be so much amused by the Oriental greeting, "We welcome you, most honorable sir, to our miserable abode," if we stopped to consider how exaggerated many of our forms of greeting, address, and compliment are.

Hyperbole can be a serviceable figure of speech if we learn to use it with restraint and for a calculated effect. Under the stress of emotion, it will slip out naturally and will then seem appropriate. If we can learn to invent fresh hyperboles, we will be able to produce the right note of emphasis (as in the first example above) or humor (as in the quotation from Aldrich).

Being related to the topic of degree, hyperbole is like the figure called **auxesis** (awk-ses'-is) (magnifying the importance or gravity of something by referring to it with a disproportionate name). So a lawyer will try to impress a jury by referring to a scratch on the arm as "a wound" or to pilfering from the petty-cash box as "embezzlement." We can accept Mark Antony's reference to the wound that Brutus inflicted on Caesar as "the most unkindest cut of all," but the occasion seemed not to warrant Senator Joseph McCarthy's classic remark, "That's the most unheard of thing I ever heard of."

Litotes (lĭ′-tə-tēz)—deliberate use of understatement, not to deceive some-one but to enhance the impressiveness of what we say.

Examples: I am a citizen of no mean city.—St. Paul

> To write is, indeed, no unpleasing employment.—Samuel Johnson, *Adventurer*, No. 138

> Last week I saw a woman flayed, and you will hardly believe how much it altered her appearance for the worse.—Jonathan Swift, *A Tale of a Tub*

> With its oratorical blast, the session filled more than 33,250 pages of the *Congressional Record*, another record which cost the taxpayers only some $3,000,000.—Article in *Time*, October 29, 1965

> Dick was awake. He was rather more than that; he and Inez were making love.—Truman Capote, *In Cold Blood*

> Entertainer Frank Sinatra isn't the slow-burn type.—Article in *Newsweek*, November 15, 1965

> It isn't very serious. I have this tiny little tumor on the brain. —J. D. Salinger, *The Catcher in the Rye*

> For four generations we've been making medicines as if people's lives depended on them.—Ad for Eli Lilly Drug Company

Litotes is a form of **meiosis** (mī-ō′-sis) (a lessening). The same lawyer whom we saw in the previous section using *auxesis* might represent another client by referring to a case of vandalism as "teenage highjinks." A rose by any other name will smell as sweet, but a crime, if referred to by a name that is not too patently disproportionate, may lose some of its heinousness.

Rhetorical Question (erotema) (er-ot′-ə-ma)—asking a question, not for the purpose of eliciting an answer but for the purpose of asserting or denying something obliquely.

Examples: What! Gentlemen, was I not to foresee, or foreseeing was I not to endeavor to save you from all these multiplied mischiefs and disgraces? . . . Was I an Irishman on that day that I boldly withstood our pride? or on the day that I hung down my head and wept in shame and silence over the humiliation of Great Britain? I became unpopular in England for the one, and in Ireland for the other. What then? What obligation lay on me to be popular?—Edmund Burke, *Speech in the Electors of Bristol*

> Wasn't the cult of James a revealing symbol and symbol of an age and society which wanted to dwell like him in some false world of false art and false culture?—Maxwell Geismar, *Henry James and His Cult*

How can the poor feel they have a stake in a system which says that the rich may have due process but the poor may not? How can the uneducated have faith in a system which says that it will take advantage of them in every possible way? How can people have hope when we tell them that they have no recourse if they run afoul of the state justice system?—Senator Edward Kennedy, Senate debate on the Omnibus Crime Control and Safe Streets Act, 1968

A good student-body is perhaps the most important factor in a great university. How can you possibly make good wine from poor grapes?—Student paper

The *rhetorical question* is a common device in impassioned speeches, but it can be used too in written prose. It can be an effective persuasive device, subtly influencing the kind of response one wants to get from an audience. The manner in which the question is phrased can determine either a negative or an affirmative response. If we say, "Was this an act of heroism?" the audience will respond, in the proper context, with a negative answer. By inducing the audience to make the appropriate response, the rhetorical question can often be more effective as a persuasive device than a direct assertion would be.

Irony (ī'-rə-nē)—use of a word in such a way as to convey a meaning opposite to the literal meaning of the word.

Examples: For Brutus is an *honourable* man;
So are they all, *honourable* men.—Shakespeare, *Julius Caesar*, III, ii, 88–89

It is again objected, as a very absurd, ridiculous custom that a set of men should be suffered, much less employed and hired, to bawl one day in seven against the *lawfulness* of those methods most in use toward the pursuit of greatness, riches, and pleasure, which are the constant practice of all men alive on the other six. But this objection is, I think, a little unworthy of *so refined* an age as ours.—Swift, *Argument Against the Abolishing of Christianity*

By Spring, if God was good, all the *proud privileges* of trench lice, mustard gas, spattered brains, punctured lungs, ripped guts, asphyxiation, mud, and gangrene, might be his.—Thomas Wolfe, *Look Homeward, Angel*

Fielder smiled, "I like the English," he said. "That gives me a *nice warm* feeling," Leamas retorted.—John Le Carré, *The Spy Who Came in from the Cold*

Neither the union nor anyone else could persuade a single soul to move into this "model facility."—John Barron, article on the FHA in *Reader's Digest*, April 1966

I was simply *overjoyed* at the thought of having to leave my guy and return to school for finals.—Student paper

Sure you could live without Yellow Pages (or without newspapers or automobiles or clocks).—Bell Telephone ad

As a trope that quite definitely conveys a "transferred meaning," *irony* is related to the topic of contraries or the topic of contradiction. A highly sophisticated device, irony must be used with great caution. If you misjudge the intelligence of your audience, you may find that your audience is taking your words in their ostensible sense rather than in the intended opposite sense.

The Tudor rhetoricians had a special name for the kind of irony in which one proposed to pass over some matter, yet managed subtly to reveal the matter anyway. They called this kind of irony **paralipsis** (par-ə-lip'-sis). A notable example of *paralipsis* is found in Mark Antony's famous "Friends, Romans, countrymen" speech in *Julius Caesar*:

> Let but the commons hear this testament,
> Which (pardon me) I do not mean to read,
> And they would go and kiss dead Caesar's wounds . . .
> Have patience, gentle friends; I must not read it.
> It is not meet you know how Caesar lov'd you. . . .
> 'Tis good you know not that you are his heirs.
>
> (III, ii, 136–51)

A look at the entire speech will show how Antony, despite his disclaimers, managed to let the mob know what was in Caesar's last will.

Onomatopoeia (on-ə-mot-ə-pe'-a)—use of words whose sound echoes the sense.

Examples: 'Tis not enough no harshness gives offense,
> The sound must seem an echo to the sense:
> Soft is the strain when Zephyr gently blows,
> And the smooth stream in smoother numbers flows;
> But when loud surges lash the sounding shore,
> The hoarse, rough verse should like the torrent roar:
> When Ajax strives some rock's vast weight to throw,
> The line too labors, and the words move slow;
> Not so, when swift Camilla scours the plain,
> Flies o'er the unbending corn, and skims along the main.
>
> —Pope, *Essay on Criticism*, II, 364–73

Over the cobbles he clattered and clashed in the dark innyard.—Alfred Noyes, "The Highwayman"

Strong gongs groaning as the guns boom far.—G. K. Chesterton, *Lepanto*

My days have crackled and gone up in smoke.—Francis Thompson, "The Hound of Heaven"

A talking twitter all they had to sing.—Robert Frost, "Our Singing Strength"

The birds chirped away. Fweet, Fweet, Bootchee-Fweet.—Saul Bellow, "Masby's Memoirs," *The New Yorker*, July 20, 1968

In the passage quoted above from Pope, some of the onomatopoetic effects are produced by the rhythm of the lines as well as by the sounds of words. Since *onomatopoeia* seeks to match sound with sense, it is easy to see why this figure was commonly associated with the topic of similarity. *Onomatopoeia* will be used much less frequently in prose than in poetry, yet it still has its appropriate uses in prose. Wherever sound-effects can be used to set the emotional or ethical tone of a passage, *onomatopoeia* can make a contribution. In seeking to discredit a person or an act, we could reinforce the effect of pejorative diction with cacophony. In a phrase like "a dastardly episode," we reveal our attitude toward the event not only by the unpleasant connotations of the word *dastardly* but also by the harsh sound of the word.

Oxymoron (ok-sē-mor'-on)—the yoking of two terms that are ordinarily contradictory.

Examples: expressions like *sweet pain, cheerful pessimist, conspicuous by her absence, cruel kindness, thunderous silence, luxurious poverty, abject arrogance, make haste slowly, jumbo shrimp.*

By thus combining contradictories, writers produce a startling effect, and they may, if their *oxymorons* are fresh and apt, win for themselves a reputation for wit. There is displayed in this figure, as in most metaphorical language, what Aristotle considered a special mark of genius: the ability to see similarities. Here are some examples of *oxymoron*:

Here's much to do with hate, but more with love.
Why then, O *brawling love*! O *loving hate*!
O *anything* of *nothing* first create!
O *heavy lightness, serious vanity*!
Misshappen chaos of *well-seeming* forms!
Feather of lead, bright smoke, cold fire, sick health!
Still-waking sleep, that is not what it is!
This love I feel, that feel no love in this
             —William Shakespeare, *Romeo and Juliet*, I, i

O *miserable abundance, O beggarly riches*!
             —John Donne, *Devotions Upon Emergens Occasions*

A soul immortal, spending all her fires
Wasting her strength in *strenuous idleness*.
                    —Edward Young, *The Complaint, or Night Thoughts*

There is a sort of *dead-alive* hackneyed people about, who are scarcely conscious of living except in the exercise of some conventional occupation.—Robert Louis Stevenson, "An Apology for Idlers"

The new show at the Museum of Modern Art somehow manages to avoid *visual din.*—Aline Saarinen, a report on a showing of advertising posters on the Huntley-Brinkley show, January 24, 1968

. . . or, possibly, to a draft of Edward Kennedy, whose *absent presence* constituted one of the few phenomena here that were not familiar to those who had seen the Early Show at Miami Beach.—Richard H. Rovere, "Letter from Chicago," *The New Yorker*, September 7, 1968

The *relaxed tenseness* of the Beatles' music reflects the restlessness of the teenage generation.—Student paper

These devices were calculated to stir his audience into a *rational hysteria.*—Student paper

Closely allied to oxymoron is **paradox** (par'-ə-doks) an apparently contradictory statement that nevertheless contains a measure of truth. *Paradox* is like oxymoron in that both are built on contradictories, but paradox may not be a trope at all, because it involves not so much a "turn" of meaning in juxtaposed words as a "turn" of meaning in the whole statement. Here are some examples of *paradox*:

Art is a form of lying in order to tell the truth.—Pablo Picasso

The less we copy the renowned ancients, the more we shall resemble them.—Edward Young, *Conjectures on Original Composition*

Portnoy's Complaint, a novel in the form of a psychoanalytic monologue carried on by a guilt-ridden bachelor, is too funny not to be taken seriously.—Book review in *Time*, February 21, 1969

Professor [Harry] Levin has always in a sense suffered from the weakness of this strength.—Book review in the London *Times Literary Supplement*, September 1, 1966

He [Joseph K. in Kafka's *The Trial*] is guilty of being innocent.
—J. Mitchell Morse, article in *College English*, May, 1969

But the essence of that ugliness is the thing which will always make it beautiful.—Gertrude Stein, "How Writing Is Written"

We know too much for one to know much.—J. Robert Oppenheimer, *The Open Mind*

The past is the prologue.—Paul Newman, an NBC special "From Here to the Seventies," October 7, 1969

Concluding Remarks on the Figures of Speech

A knowledge of the figures that have been presented in this chapter will not insure that you will be able to invent your own figures or that when you use figures you will use them aptly and efficaciously. The benefit from such an investigation is rather that having been made aware of the various schemes and tropes you may make a conscious effort to use figures when you see that they will suit your purpose. In acquiring any skill, we must at first do consciously what experts do automatically; or, as Dr. Johnson said, "What we hope ever to do with ease, we must learn first to do with diligence." And during this period of apprenticeship, we can expect to do awkwardly what experts do smoothly. With practice, however, we will arrive at that happy state of naturalness that Longinus spoke of in *On the Sublime*:

> Wherefore a figure is at its best when the very fact that it is a figure escapes attention. . . . For art is perfect when it seems to be nature, and nature hits the mark when she contains art hidden within her.

Exercise

Directions: Find illustrations in twentieth-century prose or poetry of the following: (Page numbers refer to the section where the figure is discussed and illustrated.)

Schemes

Parallelism—similarity of structure in a pair of series of related words, phrases, or clauses (p. 45)

Isocolon—similarity not only of structure but of length (p. 46)

Antithesis—the juxtaposition of contrasting ideas, often in parallel structure (p. 46)

Anastrophe—inversion of the natural or usual word order (p. 47)

Parenthesis—insertion of some verbal unit in a position that interrupts the normal syntactical flow of the sentence (p. 48)

Apposition—placing side by side two co-ordinate elements, the second of which serves as an explanation or modification of the first (p. 49)

Ellipsis—the deliberate omission of a word or of words readily implied by the context (p. 50)

Asyndeton—deliberate omission of conjunctions between a series (p. 51)

Polysyndeton—deliberate use of many conjunctions (p. 52)

Alliteration—repetition of initial or medial consonants in two or more adjacent words (p. 52)

Assonance—the repetition of similar vowel forms, preceded and followed by different consonants, in the stressed syllables of adjacent words (p. 53)

Anaphora—repetition of the same word or group of words at the beginning of successive clauses (p. 54)

Epistrophe—repetition of the same word or group of words at the ends of successive clauses (p. 55)

Epanalepsis—repetition at the end of a clause of the word that occurred at the beginning of the clause (p. 56)

Anadiplosis—repetition of the last word of one clause at the beginning of the following clause (p. 56)

Climax—arrangement of words, phrases, or clauses in an order of increasing importance (p. 57)

Antimetabole—repetition of words, in successive clauses, in reverse grammatical order (p. 58)

Chiasmus—reversal of grammatical structures in successive clauses (but no repetition of words) (p. 58)

Polyptoton—repetition of words derived from the same root (p. 59)

Tropes

Metaphor—implied comparison between two things of unlike nature (p. 60)

Simile—explicit comparison between two things of unlike nature (p. 60)

Synecdoche—figure of speech in which a part stands for the whole (p. 61)

Metonymy—substitution of some attributive or suggestive word for what is actually meant (p. 62)

Antanaclasis—repetition of a word in two different senses (p. 62)

Paronomasis—use of words alike in sound but different in meaning (p. 63)

Syllepsis—use of a word understood differently in relation to two or more other words, which it modifies or governs (p. 63)

Anthimeria—the substitution of one part of speech for another (p. 64)

Periphrasis (antonomasia)—substitution of a descriptive word or phrase for a proper name or of a proper name for a quality associated with the name (p. 65)

Personification (prosopopoeia)—investing abstractions for inanimate objects with human qualities or abilities (p. 66)

Hyperbole—the use of exaggerated terms for the purpose of emphasis or heightened effect (p. 67)

Litotes—deliberate use of understatement (p. 68)

Rhetorical question—asking a question, not for the purpose of eliciting an answer but for the purpose of asserting or denying something obliquely (p. 68)

Irony—use of a word in such a way as to convey a meaning opposite to the literal meaning of the word (p. 69)

Onomatapoeia—use of words whose sound echoes the sense (p. 70)

Oxymoron—the yoking of two terms which are ordinarily contradictory (p. 71)

Paradox—an apparently contradictory statement that nevertheless contains a measure of truth (p. 72)

Imitation

Up to this point we have been dealing with the precepts of style. Now we will move on to the second of the ways in which one learns to write or to improve one's writing—imitation. Classical rhetoric books are filled with testimonies about the value of imitation for the refinement of the many skills involved in effective speaking or writing. Style is, after all, the most imitable of the skills that cooperate to produce effective discourse.

Rhetoricians recommended a variety of exercises to promote conscious imitation. Roman school children, for example, were regularly set the task of translating Greek passages into Latin and vice versa. In some of the Renaissance schools in England, students worked back and forth between Greek and Latin and English. Schoolmasters—the better ones anyway—were aware that grammatical differences among these three languages necessitated certain stylistic adjustments in the translation from one language to another. Despite these differences, however, students did learn from this exercise many valuable lessons about sentence structure.

Another exercise was the practice of paraphrasing poetry into prose. Here again many adjustments in style had to be made. Besides teaching students the salient differences between the poetic medium and the prose medium, this exercise made students pay close attention to the potentialities of precise, concrete diction, of emphatic disposition of words, and of figures of speech. Even today there are those who maintain that the best way to improve one's prose style is to study or write poetry.

Another common practice was to set the students the task of saying something in a variety of ways. This process usually started out with a model sentence, which had to be converted into a variety of forms each retaining the basic thought of the original. Erasmus, for instance, in Chapter 33 of his widely-used little book, *De duplici copia verborum ac rerum,* showed the students 150 ways of phrasing the Latin sentence, *Tuae literae me magnopere delectarunt* (Your letter has delighted me very much). This variety was achieved partly by the choice of different words, partly by different collocations of words. Here, in English, is a sampling of Erasmus's reworkings:

> Your epistle has cheered me greatly.
>
> Your note has been the occasion of unusual pleasure for me.
>
> When your letter came, I was seized with an extraordinary pleasure.
>
> What you wrote to me was most delightful.
>
> On reading your letter, I was filled with joy.
>
> Your letter provided me with no little pleasure.

Obviously, not all of the 150 sentences were equally satisfactory or appropriate; in fact, some were monstrosities. But by artificially experimenting with various forms, students became aware of the flexibility of the language in which they were working and learned to extend their own range. Ultimately they learned that although there is a variety of ways of saying something, there is a "best way" for their particular subject matter, occasion, or audience. What was "best" for one occasion or audience, they discovered, is not "best" for another occasion or audience.

This text will give you the opportunity to practice two kinds of imitation—copying passages of prose and imitating various sentence patterns. But before we get into those exercises, we will present the testimony of some famous writers about how they learned to write. You will see as you read these testimonies how basic imitation is to the formation of style.

Testimonies about the Value of Imitation

Malcolm X

I saw that the best thing I could do was get hold of a dictionary—to study, to learn some words. I was lucky enough to reason also that I should try to improve my penmanship. It was sad. I couldn't even write in a straight line. It was both ideas together that moved me to request a dictionary along with some tables and pencils from the Norfolk Prison Colony school.

I spent two days just riffling uncertainly through the dictionary's pages. I'd never realized so many words existed! I didn't know *which* words I needed to learn. Finally, just to start some kind of action, I began copying.

In my slow, painstaking, ragged handwriting, I copied into my tablet everything printed on that first page, down to the punctuation marks.

I believe it took me a day. Then, aloud, I read back, to myself, everything I'd written on the table. Over and over, aloud, to myself, I read my own handwriting.

I woke up the next morning, thinking about those words—immensely proud to realize that not only had I written so much at one time, but I'd written words that I never knew were in the world. Moreover, with a little effort, I also could remember what many of these words meant. I reviewed the words whose meanings I didn't remember. Funny thing, from the dictionary first page right now, that "aardvark" springs to my mind. The dictionary had a picture of it, a long-tailed, long-eared, burrowing African mammal, which lives off termites caught by sticking out its tongue as an anteater does for ants.

I was so fascinated that I went on—I copied the dictionary's next page. And the same experience came when I studied that. With every succeeding page, I also learned of people and places and events from history. Actually the dictionary is like a miniature encyclopedia. Finally the dictionary's A section had filled a whole tablet—and I went on into the B's. That was the way I started copying what eventually became the entire dictionary. It went a lot faster after so much practice helped me to pick up handwriting speed. Between what I wrote in my tablet, and writing letters, during the rest of my time in prison I would guess I wrote a million words.

From *The Autobiography of Malcolm X*, Grove Press Paperback Edition, 1966, p. 172. Reprinted by permission of Grove Press, Inc. Copyright © 1964 by Alex Haley and Malcolm X. Copyright © 1965 by Alex Haley and Betty Shabazz.

Benjamin Franklin

About this time I met with an odd volume of the *Spectator*. It was the third. I had never before seen any of them. I bought it, read it over and over, and was much delighted with it. I thought the writing excellent, and wished, if possible, to imitate it. With this view I took some of the papers, and, making short hints of the sentiment in each sentence, laid them by a few days, and then, without looking at the book, try'd to compleat the papers again, by expressing each hinted sentiment at length, and as fully as it had been expressed before, in any suitable words that should come to hand. Then I compared my *Spectator* with the original, discovered some of my faults, and corrected them. But I found I wanted a stock of words, or a readiness in recollecting and using them, which I thought I should have acquired before that time if I had gone on making verses; since the continual occasion for words of the same import, but of different length, to suit the measure, or of different sound for the rhyme, would have laid me under a constant necessity of searching for variety, and also have tended to fix that variety in my mind, and make me master of it. Therefore I took some of the tales and turned them into verse; and, after a time, when I had pretty well forgotten the prose, turned them back again. I also sometimes jumbled my collections of hints into confusion, and after some weeks endeavored to reduce them into the best order, before I began to form the full sentences and compleat the paper. This was to teach me method in the arrangement of thoughts. By comparing my work afterwards with the original, I discovered many faults and amended them; but I sometimes had the pleasure of fancying that, in certain particulars of small import, I had been lucky enough to improve the method or the language, and this encouraged me to think I might possibly in time come to be a tolerable English writer, of which I was extremely ambitious.

From *The Autobiography of Benjamin Franklin*, 1771.

Winston S. Churchill

I continued in this unpretentious situation for nearly a year. However, by being so long in the lowest form [at Harrow] I gained an immense advantage over the cleverer boys. They all went on to learn Latin and Greek and splendid things like that. But I was taught English. We were considered such dunces that we could learn only English. Mr. Somervell—a most delightful man, to whom my debt is great—was charged with the duty of teaching the stupidest boys the most disregarded thing—namely, to write mere English. He knew how to do it. He taught it as no one else has ever taught it. Not only did we learn English parsing thoroughly, but we also practised continually English analysis. Mr. Somervell had a system of his own. He took a fairly long sentence and broke it up into its components by means of black, red, blue, and green inks. Subject, verb, object: Relative Clauses, Conditional Clauses, Conjunctive and Disjunctive Clauses! Each had its colour and its bracket. It was a kind of drill. We did it almost daily. As I remained in the Third Form (ß) three times as long as anyone else, I had three times as much of it. I learned it thoroughly. Thus I got into my bones the essential structure of the ordinary British sentence—which is a noble thing. And when in after years my schoolfellows who had won prizes and distinction for writing such beautiful Latin poetry and pithy Greek epigrams had to come down again to common English, to earn their living or make their way, I did not feel myself at any disadvantage. Naturally I am biased in favour of boys learning English. I would make them all learn English: and then I would let the clever ones learn Latin as an honour, and Greek as a treat. But the only thing I would whip them for is not knowing English, I would whip them hard for that.

From *My Early Life: A Roving Commission* by Winston Churchill. Copyright 1930 Charles Scribner's Sons; copyright renewed © 1958 Winston Churchill. Reprinted with permission of Charles Scribner's Sons, an imprint of Macmillan Publishing Company.

Somerset Maugham

IX

As it is, I have had to teach myself. I have looked at the stories I wrote when I was very young in order to discover what natural aptitude I had, my original stock-in-trade, before I developed it by taking thought. The manner had a superciliousness that perhaps my years excused and an irascibility that was a defect of nature; but I am speaking now only of the way in which I expressed myself. It seems to me that I had a natural lucidity and a knack for writing easy dialogue.

When Henry Arthur Jones, then a well-known playwright, read my first novel, he told a friend that in due course I should be one of the most successful dramatists of the day. I suppose he saw in it directness and an effective way of presenting a sense that suggested a sense of the theatre. My language was commonplace, my vocabulary limited, my grammar shaky and my phrases hackneyed. But to write was an instinct that seemed as natural to me as to breathe, and I did not stop to consider if I wrote well or badly. It was not till some years later that it dawned upon me that it was a delicate art that must be painfully acquired. The discovery was forced upon me by the difficulty I found in getting my meaning down on paper. I wrote dialogue fluently, but when it came to a page of description I found myself entangled in all sorts of quandaries. I would struggle for a couple of hours over two or three sentences that I could in no way manage to straighten out. I made up my mind to teach myself how to write. Unfortunately I had no one to help me. I made many mistakes. If I had had someone to guide me like the

From *The Summing Up* by W. Somerset Maugham. Copyright 1938 by W. Somerset Maugham. Reprinted by permission of A. P. Watt Limited.

charming don of whom I spoke just now I might have been saved much
time. Such a one might have told me that such gifts as I had lay in one direction and that they must be cultivated in that direction; it was useless to
try to do something for which I had no aptitude. But at that time a florid
prose was admired. Richness of texture was sought by means of a jewelled
phrase and sentences stiff with exotic epithets: the ideal was a brocade so
heavy with gold that it stood up by itself. The intelligent young read Walter Pater with enthusiasm. My common sense suggested to me that it was
anaemic stuff; behind those elaborate, gracious periods I was conscious of a
tired, wan personality. I was young, lusty and energetic; I wanted fresh air,
action, violence, and I found it hard to breathe that dead, heavily scented
atmosphere and sit in those hushed rooms in which it was indecorous to
speak above a whisper. But I would not listen to my common sense. I persuaded myself that this was the height of culture and turned a scornful
shoulder on the outside world where men shouted and swore, played the
fool, wenched and got drunk. I read *Intentions* and *The Picture of Dorian
Gray*. I was intoxicated by the colour and rareness of the fantastic words
that thickly stud the pages of *Salome*. Shocked by the poverty of my own
vocabulary, I went to the British Museum with pencil and paper and noted
down the names of curious jewels, the Byzantine hues of old enamels, the
sensual feel of textiles, and made elaborate sentences to bring them in. Fortunately I could never find an opportunity to use them, and they lie there
yet in an old notebook ready for anyone who has a mind to write nonsense.
It was generally thought then that the Authorized Version of the Bible was
the greatest piece of prose that the English language has produced. I read
it diligently, especially the Song of Solomon, jotting down for future
use turns of phrase that struck me and making lists of unusual or beautiful words. I studied Jeremy Taylor's *Holy Dying*. In order to assimilate
his style I copied out passages and then tried to write them down from
memory.

The first fruit of this labour was a little book about Andalusia called *The
Land of the Blessed Virgin*. I had occasion to read parts of it the other day. I
know Andalusia a great deal better now than I knew it then, and I have
changed my mind about a good many things of which I wrote. Since it has
continued in America to have a small sale it occurred to me that it might be
worth while to revise it. I soon saw that this was impossible. The book was
written by someone I have completely forgotten. It bored me to distraction.
But what I am concerned with is the prose, for it was as an exercise in style
that I wrote it. It is wistful, allusive, and elaborate. It has neither ease nor
spontaneity. It smells of hothouse plants and Sunday dinner like the air in
the greenhouse that leads one of the dining-room of a big house in Bayswa-
ter. There are a great many melodious adjectives. The vocabulary is senti-
mental. It does not remind one of an Italian brocade, with its rich pattern of
gold, but of a curtain material designed by Burne-Jones and reproduced by
Morris.

x

I do not know whether it was a subconscious feeling that this sort of writing
was contrary to my bent or a naturally methodical cast of mind that led me
then to turn my attention to the writers of the Augustan Period. The prose
of Swift enchanted me. I made up my mind that this was a perfect way to
write, and I started to work on him in the same way as I had done with Jeremy Taylor. I chose *The Tale of a Tub*. It is said that when the Dean re-read it
in his old age he cried: "What genius I had then!' To my mind his genius
was better shown in other works. It is a tiresome allegory, and the irony is
facile. But the style is admirable. I cannot imagine that English can be better
written. Here are no flowery periods, fantastic turns of phrase or high-flown
images. It is a civilized prose, natural, discreet and pointed. There is no attempt to surprise by an extravagant vocabulary. It looks as though Swift
made do with the first word that came to hand, but since he had an acute
and logical brain it was always the right one, and he put it in the right place.
The strength and balance of his sentences are due to an exquisite taste. As I
had done before, I copied passages and then tried to write them out again
from memory. I tried altering words or the order in which they were set. I
found that the only possible words were those Swift had used and that the
order in which he had placed them was the only possible order. It is an im-
peccable prose.

But perfection has one grave defect: it is apt to be dull. Swift's prose is like
a French canal, bordered with poplars, that runs through a gracious and un-
dulating country. Its tranquil charm fills you with satisfaction, but it neither
excites the emotions nor stimulates the imagination. You go on and on and
presently you are a trifle bored. So, much as you may admire Swift's wonderful lucidity, his terseness, his naturalness, his lack of affectation, you find
your attention wandering after a while unless his matter peculiarly interests
you. I think if I had my time over again I would give to the prose of Dryden
the close study I gave to that of Swift. I did not come across it till I had lost
the inclination to take so much pains. The prose of Dryden is delicious. It
has not the perfection of Swift nor the easy elegance of Addison, but it has a
springtime gaiety, a conversational ease, a blithe spontaneousness that are
enchanting. Dryden was a very good poet, but it is not the general opinion
that he had a lyrical quality; it is strange that it is just this that sings in his
softly sparkling prose. Prose had never been written in England like that before; it has seldom been written like that since. Dryden flourished at a happy
moment. He had in his bones the sonorous periods and the baroque massive-
ness of Jacobean language, and under the influence of the nimble and well-
bred felicity that he learnt from the French he turned it into an instrument
that was fit not only for solemn themes but also to express the light thought
of the passing moment. He was the first of the rococo artists. If Swift re-
minds you of a French canal Dryden recalls an English river winding its
cheerful way round hills, through quietly busy towns and by nestling vil-

lages, pausing now in a noble reach and then running powerfully through a woodland country. It is alive, varied, windswept; and it has the pleasant open-air smell of England.

The work I did was certainly very good for me. I began to write better; I did not write well. I wrote stiffly and self-consciously. I tried to get a pattern into my sentences, but did not see that the pattern was evident. I took care how I placed my words, but did not reflect that an order that was natural at the beginning of the eighteenth century was most unnatural at the beginning of ours. My attempt to write in the manner of Swift made it impossible for me to achieve the effect of inevitable rightness that was just what I so much admired in him. I then wrote a number of plays and ceased to occupy myself with anything but dialogue. It was not till five years had passed that I set out again to write a novel. By then I no longer had any ambition to be a stylist; I put aside all thought of fine writing. I wanted to write without any frills of language, in as bare and unaffected a manner as I could. I had so much to say that I could afford to waste no words. I wanted merely to set down the facts. I began with the impossible aim of using no adjectives at all. I thought that if you could find the exact term a qualifying epithet could be dispensed with. As I saw it in my mind's eye my book would have the appearance of an immensely long telegram in which for economy's sake you had left out every word that was not necessary to make the sense clear. I have not read it since I corrected the proofs and do not know how near I came to doing what I tried. My impression is that it is written at least more naturally than anything I had written before; but I am sure that it is often slipshod, and I daresay there are in it a good many mistakes in grammar.

Since then I have written many other books; and though ceasing my methodical study of the old masters (for though the spirit is willing, the flesh is weak), I have continued with increasing assiduity to try to write better. I discovered my limitations, and it seemed to me that the only sensible thing was to aim at what excellence I could within them. I knew that I had no lyrical quality. I had a small vocabulary, and no efforts that I could make to enlarge it much availed me. I had little gift of metaphor; the original and striking simile seldom occurred to me. Poetic flights and the great imaginative sweep were beyond my powers. I could admire them in others as I could admire their far-fetched tropes and the unusual but suggestive language in which they clothed their thoughts, but my own invention never presented me with such embellishments; and I was tired of trying to do what did not come easily to me. On the other hand, I had an acute power of observation, and it seemed to me that I could see a great many things that other people missed. I could put down in clear terms what I saw. I had a logical sense, and if not great feeling for the richness and strangeness of words, at all events a lively appreciation of their sound. I know that I should never write as well as I could wish, but I thought with pains I could arrive at writing a well as my natural defects allowed. On taking thought it seemed to me that I must aim at lucidity, simplicity, and euphony. I have put these three qualities in the order of the importance I assigned to them.

Rollo Walter Brown: How the French Boy Learns to Write

As soon as an American teacher comes into direct contact with the French educational system, he marvels at the large place writing holds in the schools and their routine life. First, it matters not in what classroom a small boy may be seen, he is never without his general notebook, in which he records all assignments, all problems, all experiments, all quotations to be learned, all geographical and historical notes and maps, as well as many special exercises; and the language he employs in this work is carefully marked and graded by the teacher. In the second place, compositions are numerous. From the time the boy is regarded as mature enough to think consecutively, he prepares compositions at regular intervals. In some classes he writes two short exercises every three or five days. In the elementary primary schools, even up to the time the boy is thirteen or fourteen years old, the shorter themes once or twice a week seem to stand in great favor. These vary in length, usually, from a hundred and fifty to four hundred words—they are rather longer than the average American daily theme—and the less frequent, longer compositions range ordinarily from six hundred to fifteen hundred words. Then, in the upper grades, there are, in addition, many papers in history, civics, philosophy, and literature. So it may be seen that a boy is provided with much opportunity to write. It is, in fact, scarcely an exaggeration to say that he writes all the time. In any event, his practice is so continuous that he sooner or later comes to do the work in a perfectly normal frame of mind, just as he performs his other schoolday labors.

The volume of required writing, however, is regarded or less important than its quality. If a boy thinks and writes poorly, he is looked upon as an unfortunate who deserves either pity or contempt. If, on the other hand, he is able to think and write skillfully, he is held in great honor by his teachers and his classmates. And this interest in ability to write is evident outside the recitation-room. Authors of books and articles discuss the perils of the pure mother tongue as seriously as if they were dealing with a question of ethics or of grave national policy. Parents, I found when I was securing compositions for the purpose of this book, are usually desirous of preserving the written work of their children. Moreover, when pupils distinguish themselves in examinations—which in France are always largely a matter of composition—they receive prizes and public mention very much as if they were the winners of athletic trophies. Now I would not have anyone make the hasty inference that intellectual contests are substituted for athletics. The French boy loves the open just as much as the American boy does, and outdoor sports are steadily taking a larger place in school life. But the ideal of writing well has been held up before the schoolboy so long, and with such seriousness, that he attaches more importance to ability of this kind than the average American boy could at present be led to comprehend.

When so much importance is everywhere attached to ability to write, it is not surprising to find that in both the primary and secondary school systems the course in the mother tongue gives large place to systematic training in composition. It is the conviction of the great body of teachers, as well as the Ministry, that work in grammar, rhetoric, and literature is in most respects lost unless it contributes to the pupil's ability to give full, intelligent expression to his thought. Moreover, theories of teaching, and all the proposed changes in the course of study, seem to be considered first in respect to their influence on this ability of the pupil. Expression is not the sole end, but in all the lower schools it is the primary end. And, taking the other point of view, the chief responsibility for the pupil's manner of expression rests upon the teacher of the mother tongue. As we shall see later, the writing that the boy does in history, geometry, and his other subjects is made to contribute its full share to his skill; yet upon the teacher of the native language rests the largest responsibility and the greatest burden of labor. He accepts his task as difficult, very expensive in time and energy, but extremely important. Without going into any examination of exceptional aims or of intricate personal devices, let us see what he attempts to accomplish and how he pursues his way.

Two groups of exercises are everywhere regarded as essential preliminaries to work in original composition. Those in the first group are intended to enlarge and organize the pupil's vocabulary. Now, I am aware that when one stands apart and looks at exercises designed to improve the vocabulary, they are likely to appear very artificial and ineffective. And, in truth, they may be. In the hands of a poorly trained teacher, or one who lacks the all-important teaching instinct, it would be difficult to imagine an exercise that could be more dismally futile. But this possibility seems to be disregarded by French educators. They are ready to admit that the lessons may become valueless, or even harmful, when directed by a poor teacher—and what exercise may not?—but they do not spring to the conclusion that such lessons should for that reason be cast aside. They have taken the good teacher as the norm, and have given themselves earnestly to the task of obviating the dangers and developing the advantages of a kind of instruction which at its best appears to them to have unquestioned value.

The theory upon which this instruction is based is not the individual opinion of the occasional teacher; it is accepted doctrine throughout the country. In the volume of *Instructions* issued by the Minister to teachers in the secondary school system, it is summarized as follows: "The preceding exercises [in grammar] help the pupil to understand his native language and to enrich his vocabulary; but for this latter purpose, one ought not to rely solely upon them or even upon conversation, dictations, reading, or the explication of texts. The pupil must learn words, though never apart from things; he must be able to seize their signification and the exact shade of their meaning; and he must become accustomed to finding the words quickly when he stands in need. Hence the value of exercises devoted especially to the study of the vocabulary."

The teaching of the vocabulary I found, then, falls readily into three parts: (1) enlarging; (2) sharpening; (3) quickening. To be sure, the instruction is not divided into three separate processes, but the teacher has a threefold aim that determines his method. One will not see every aspect of the method in one recitation or in several. Yet the principles emphasized in the *Instructions* to secondary teachers, in textbooks for primary schools, in classes in the mother tongue in both school systems, and even in many classes in English, serve to give outline to the varying details of the work.

In the exercise designed to enlarge the vocabulary, it is held to be absolutely essential that the pupil relate the word unmistakably to the object or idea which it represents. Although it is much more difficult to have a word in mind without relating it to some idea than we generally suppose, the French teacher seems to take no risk. He guides the pupil to feel the uselessness of words unless they are symbols of something physically or mentally real. Secondly, the pupil is required to relate a new word to other words already in his working vocabulary, so that it will remain firmly fixed in his mind. The new word may be linked to a synonym that is known to the pupil, it may be contrasted with words already known to him, or it simply may be linked to a group of ideas that by circumstances are brought to his mind frequently; but in some manner he is led to associate it with words which he knows well. Thirdly, the word is put into normal contexts—sometimes before its meanings are explained—so that the pupil may develop a feeling for its idiomatic use. And finally, in the definition or explanation that a word or a group of words may require, the beginning is specific rather than general, concrete rather than abstract. In theory at least, a teacher would establish the meaning of *sincere* in a boy's mind before he discussed the abstract quality, *sincerity*. He would show the boy that many things are *rich* before he explained *richness;* or *noble,* before he explained *nobility*. Moreover, if a word has many definitions, the simplest one, the one most easily understood, the one that would most readily associate itself with the boy's stock of concrete ideas and images is explained before those that are predominantly abstract or figurative. It is taken for granted that if a word is to be of much value to a boy, it must represent an idea clearly established in his mind, and it must have its individual flavor.

. . .

In the exercises designed primarily to sharpen feeling for words, one is sure to be impressed with the many means by which a word is brought into the pupil's life. He defines it, he finds examples of its accepted uses, he learns its original significance—its literal meaning when the word is predominately figurative—he compares it with other words of similar meaning, and above all, he contrasts it with words that are essentially its opposite. It is scarcely too much to say that the basis of all word-teaching is contrast rather than likeness. If a given word is used chiefly as a noun, the teacher does not let the pupil form the notion that synonymous adjectives may be attached to it indiscriminately, but helps him to learn what adjectives are or may be used appropriately with it. If the word is an adjective or verb, he shows how it normally takes certain adverbs, and how others, as soon as they are brought into close relation with it, seem awkward and unidiomatic. In a similar manner he guides the pupil to see the distinctions that usage has established between nouns which in general meaning are the same. To take a very simple example, if the word *stem* appeared in a lesson, he would be extremely careful to bring out the difference between *stem* and *stalk, stem* and *trunk,* and *stalk* and *trunk,* so that the pupil would never fall into the error of using them as if they were convertible terms. Through numerous exercises of this kind the pupil is made to see that words do not have the same value, and that the choosing of them is not merely a question of finding approved dictionary definitions when occasion arises, but of possessing a word sense.

Concerning the exercises in calling words to mind quickly, little need be said. Their character has already been suggested. They usually consist of rapid-fire questions about the word itself, its use, its like and opposites, and of oral or written practice in composition on subjects likely to call words of a given class into use. I saw no turning of verse into prose, but I did see many exercises that required the pupils to turn one kind of prose into another. In most instances the teacher simply read a story or an essay to the class and then called upon pupils to repeat it in language of their own. After a little practice of this kind, a boy unconsciously adopts many words that he has well understood but has not made a part of his working vocabulary. He does not surrender his individuality, as he must do—momentarily, at least—in writing imitations, yet he is in a state of open-mindedness that encourages a definite impression of what he reads or hears read.

The scope of the lessons in vocabulary is wide. By the time a boy has reached the age of twelve he not only has had practice in calling simple objects by their right names, but he has reached out into the world around him and made acquaintance with words belonging to a great variety of activities. He can speak intelligently about the professions, the occupations of workingmen, the farm, social life, political life; he can discuss the more familiar phenomena of the atmosphere, the physical qualities of his friends, their moral virtues and their moral faults; he can use accurately the words that spring from such relations as commerce, war, colonization, life in the city or the small village; and he can talk or write about such means of communication as railways, steamships, street-railways, and the telegraph and telephone. This ability he gains not by sporadic or blind plunging about, but by means of orderly, systematic study. The instruction is not overrigid or mechanical; one might visit classrooms for months without feeling that the instruction was organized in any large way. Yet it is the careful organization that makes the wide scope of the work possible. The simplicity is not that of isolated, individual effort, but of well-designed plan.

. . .

The second of the preliminary exercises universally employed by the French teacher of the mother tongue is dictation. In America, dictation seems to have been put aside to make way for something new. French teachers, however, do not hesitate to use an old-fashioned method or device if they believe it is good. Instead, therefore, of dropping dictation from the programme of studies, they have emphasized it and developed it until it is now a very important and thoroughly established part of their educational procedure. It is based on the conviction that a child can acquire skill before he develops the power of profound or sustained thought. He has much practice, then, in writing the thoughts of others while he is yet too young to write his own. Teachers admit that dictation has its dangers, but since they regard these as incomparable to its possible value, they employ it, just as they employ exercises in vocabulary, with the confidence that though they are risking small dangers, they are following the direction of a larger common sense.

French teachers usually dwell upon four or five specific values of dictation. It gives the pupil much practice in the handling of the sentence; it directs his attention to grammatical constructions; it helps him to learn to spell, to punctuate, and to capitalize; it enlarges his vocabulary and gives him practice in the use of words already known to him; and it fills his mind with good standards of speech. To these should be added one value that the thoughtful teacher must regard as greatest of all; namely, that dictation prevents the pupil from separating spoken language and writing. One of the objections almost invariably made by the young pupil to practice in original composition is that writing seems an artificial process quite unlike anything he has ever before attempted. In making this objection, he is, of course, merely giving expression to the fact that language is naturally a matter of speech rather than writing, and the additional fact that he has not felt a close relation between what he says by word of mouth and what he writes on paper. If then, before he begins composition, and later while he is practicing it in an elementary manner, he has drill in writing down what he hears, the relation between speech and writing is much less likely to be weakened. While he is listening carefully to his teacher's reading, catching the words in their natural thought groups, and putting them down one by one in his exercise-book, he is not only learning much about the mechanics of composition, but he is saving himself from the error of looking upon theme-writing as something far removed from normal existence.

In giving dictations, the teacher exercises great care. After the very earliest classes, where the work must of necessity be simple, he does not give isolated or detached sentences, but instead, a complete, interesting paragraph. Moreover, he always explains the paragraph fully before he asks the pupil to write it down. This precaution is regarded as so important that a teacher is prohibited from requiring a pupil to write down anything that is meaningless or vague. Again, he reads a paragraph that contains material suited to keep the pupil's attention. That is to say, the ideas and the words in which they are expressed must be just within the pupil's reach. And finally, the teacher guards against letting the exercise become monotonous. It is never long usually it is a short, crisp paragraph—the corrections are made immediately while interest is warm, and the pupil is not asked to rewrite the diction unless he has been exceedingly careless. The ten or fifteen minutes are so full of pleasant activity that the time passes quickly, and the boy seems never to dream that he is doing something that might, under a thoughtless teacher, become a dreary, useless punishment.

Summary

The attention, then, that the actual business of writing receives in the French schools is a matter not only of adequate instruction, but of full and definite practice under stimulating circumstances. Composition is held up as a very important part—in fact, the most important part—of the course in the mother tongue. Studies in vocabulary and practice in dictation are carried on constantly in the lower grades in order that the boy may express himself without hindrance when he is once old enough to have something of his own to say in organized compositions. The material assigned is regarded as a matter of great moment. It is intended to develop, in order, the powers of attention and observation, the imagination, and habits of reflection. This material, moreover, is almost invariably discussed in the classroom until the pupil is awakened and interested; and when he writes upon it, he must give the most thoughtful care to organization and general good form. In the criticism of themes, oral discussion holds a large place. Furthermore, the teacher makes his critical suggestions distinctly constructive; that is, he emphasizes the difference between poor work and good, and he leads the pupils to reflect upon the possibilities that the subject-matter possesses, rather than upon the magnitude of their own shortcomings. And finally, the training that pupils receive in the study of the mother tongue is re-enforced to no small degree by the work in other subjects.

Exercises in Imitation

Copying Passages

The first exercise in imitation that we will recommend to you consists of copying passages, word for word, from admired authors. This may strike you as being a rather brainless exercise, but it can teach you a great deal about the niceties of style. Earlier in this chapter, we pointed out a number of features one looks for when one makes a close study of style. These features will strike you as you carefully transcribe the passage.

If you are to derive any benefit from this exercise, you must observe a few simple rules.

1. You must not spend more than fifteen or twenty minutes copying at any one time. If you extend this exercise much beyond twenty minutes at any one sitting, your attention will begin to wander, and you will find yourself merely copying words.

2. You must do this copying with a pencil or pen. Typing is so fast and so mechanical that you can copy off whole passages without paying any attention to the features of an author's style. Copying by hand, you transcribe the passage at such a pace that you have time to observe the choice and disposition of words, the patterns of sentences, and the length and variety of sentences.

3. You must not spend too much time with any one author. If you concentrate on a single author's style, you may find yourself falling into that "servile imitation" that rhetoricians warned of. The aim of this exercise is not to acquire someone else's style but to lay the groundwork for developing your own style by getting the "feel" of a variety of styles.

4. You must read the entire passage before starting to copy it so that you can capture the thought and the manner of the passage as a whole. When you are copying, it is advisable to read each sentence through before transcribing it. After you have finished copying the passage, you should read your transcription so that you once again get a sense of the passage as a whole.

5. You must copy the passage slowly and accurately. If you are going to dash through this exercise, you might as well not do it at all. A mechanical way of insuring accuracy and the proper pace is to make your handwriting as legible as you can.

You will derive the maximum benefit from this copying exercise if you practice it over an extended period of time. Transcribing a single different passage every day for a month will prove more beneficial to you than transcribing several different pages every day for a week. You must have time to absorb what you have been observing in this exercise; and you will not have time to absorb the many lessons to be learned from this exercise if you cram it into a short period.

Specimen Passages for Imitation

The Bible

I returned and saw under the sun that the race is not to the swift, nor the battle to the strong, neither yet bread to the wise, nor yet riches to men of

understanding, not yet favour to men of skill; but time and chance hap-
peneth to them all. For man also knoweth not his time: as the fishes that are
taken in an evil net, and as the birds that are caught in the snare; so are the
sons of men snared in an evil time, when it falleth suddenly upon them. This
wisdom have I seen also under the sun, and it seemed great unto me. There
was a little city, and few men within it; and there came a great king against
it, and besieged it, and built great bulwarks against it. Now there was found
in it a poor wise man, and he by his wisdom delivered the city; yet no man
remembered that same poor man. Then said I, Wisdom is better than
strength: nevertheless the poor man's wisdom is despised, and his words are
not heard. The words of wise men are heard in quiet more than the cry of
him that ruleth among fools. Wisdom is better than weapons of war: but one
sinner destroyeth much good.

From Ecclesiastes, IX, 11–18, King James Version, 1611.

And so it was, that, while they were there, the days were accomplished that
she should be delivered. And she brought forth her firstborn son and
wrapped him in swaddling clothes and laid him in a manger; because there
was no room for them in the inn. And there were in the same country shep-
herds abiding in the field, keeping watch over their flock by night. And, lo,
the angel of the Lord came upon them, and the glory of the Lord shone
round about them: and they were sore afraid. And the angel said unto them,
Fear not: for, behold, I bring you good tidings of great joy, which shall be to
all people. For unto you is born this day in the city of David a Saviour, which
is Christ the Lord. And this shall be a sign unto you; Ye shall find the babe
wrapped in swaddling clothes, lying in a manger. And suddenly there was
with the angel a multitude of the heavenly host praising God and saying,
Glory to God in the highest, and on earth peace, good will toward men.

From St. Luke, II, 6–14, King James Version, 1611.

Sir Thomas Browne

If the nearness of our last necessity brought a nearer conformity into it, there
were a happiness in hoary hairs, and no calamity in half-senses. But the long
habit of living indisposeth us for dying; when avarice makes us the sport of
death, when even David grew politically cruel, and Solomon could hardly be
said to be the wisest of men. But many are too early old, and before the date
of age. Adversity stretcheth our days, misery makes Alcmena's nights, and
time hath no wings unto it. But the most tedious being is that which can un-
wish itself, content to be nothing, or never to have been, which was beyond
the malcontent of Job, who cursed not the day of his life, but his nativity;
content to have so far been, as to have a title to future being, although he had
lived here but in an hidden state of life, and as it were an abortion.

From *Hydriotaphia, Urn-Burial,* 1658.

John Dryden

'Tis a vanity common to all writers, to overvalue their own productions; and 'tis better for me to own this failing in myself, than the world to do it for me. For what other reason have I spent my life in so unprofitable a study? why am I grown old in seeking so barren a reward as fame? The same parts and application which have made me a poet might have raised me to any honours of the grown, which are often given to men of as little learning and less honesty than myself. No Government has ever been, or ever can be, wherein time-servers and blockheads will not be uppermost. The persons are only changed, but the same jugglings in State, the same hypocrisy in religion, the same self-interest and mismanagement, will remain for ever. Blood and money will be lavished in all ages, only for the preferment of new faces, with old consciences. There is too often a jaundice in the eyes of great men; they see not those whom they raise in the same colours with other men. All whom they affect look golden to them, when the gilding is only in their own distempered sight. These considerations have given me a kind of contempt for those who have risen by unworthy ways. I am not ashamed to be little, when I see them so infamously great; neither do I know why the name of poet should be dishonourable to me, if I am truly one, as I hope I am; for I will never do anything that shall dishonour it.

From the Dedication to *Examen Poeticum*, 1693.

Daniel Defoe

I must confess myself to have been very much dejected just before this happened; for the prodigious number that were taken sick the week or two before, besides those that died, was such, and the lamentations were so great everywhere, that a man must have seemed to have acted even against his reason if he had so much as expected to escape; and as there was hardly a house but mine in all my neighbourhood but what was infected, so had it gone on it would not have been long that there would have been any more neighbours to be infected. Indeed it is hardly credible what dreadful havoc the last three weeks had made, for if I might believe the person whose calculations I always found very well grounded, there were not less than 30,000 people dead and near 100,000 fallen sick in the three weeks I speak of; for the number that sickened was surprising; indeed it was astonishing, and those whose courage upheld them all the time before, sank under it now.

In the middle of their distress, when the condition of the City of London was so truly calamitous, just then it pleased God, as it were, by His immediate hand to disarm this·enemy; the poison was taken out of the sting. It was wonderful; even the physicians themselves were surprised at it. Wherever they visited they found their patients better; either they had sweated kindly, or the tumors were broke, or the carbuncles went down, and the inflammations round them changed color, or the fever was gone, or the violent headache was assuaged, or some good symptom was in the case; so that in a few days everybody was recovering, whole families that were infected and down, that had ministers praying with them, and expected death every hour, were revived and healed, and none died at all out of them.

From *A Journal of the Plague Year,* 1722.

Lady Mary Wortley Montagu

This little digression has interrupted my telling you we passed over the fields of Carlowitz, where the last great victory was obtained by Prince Eugene over the Turks. The marks of that glorious bloody day are yet recent, the field being strewed with the skulls and carcasses of unburied men, horses, and camels. I could not look without horror, on such numbers of mangled human bodies, and reflect on the injustice of war, that makes murder not only necessary but meritorious. Nothing seems to me a plainer proof of the irrationality of mankind (whatever fine claims we pretend to reason) than the rage with which they contest for a small spot of ground, when such vast parts of fruitful earth lie quite uninhabited. It is true, custom has now made it unavoidable; but can there be a greater demonstration of want of reason, than a custom being firmly established, so plainly contrary to the interest of man in general? I am a good deal inclined to believe Mr. Hobbes, that the state of nature is a state of war; but thence I conclude human nature is not rational, if the word reason means common sense, as I suppose it does. I have a great many admirable arguments to support this reflection; but I won't trouble you with them, but return, in a plain style, to the history of my travels.

From a letter to Alexander Pope on February 12, 1717,
Old Style, from Belgrade.

Edward Gibbon

The renewal, or perhaps the improvement, of my English life was embittered by the alteration of my own feelings. At the age of twenty-one I was, in my proper station of a youth, delivered from the yoke of education, and delighted with the comparative state of liberty and affluence. My filial obedience was natural and easy; and in the gay prospect of futurity, my ambition did not extend beyond the enjoyment of my books, my leisure, and my patrimonial estate, undisturbed by the cares of a family and the duties of a profession. But in the militia I was armed with power; in my travels, I was exempt from control; and as I approached, as I gradually passed, my thirtieth year, I began to feel the desire of being master in my own house. The most gentle authority will sometimes frown without reason, the most cheerful submission will sometimes murmur without cause; and such is the law of our imperfect nature that we must either command or obey; that our personal liberty is supported by the obsequiousness of our own dependents. While so many of my acquaintances were married or in parliament, or advancing with a rapid step in the various roads of honour and fortune, I stood alone, immovable and insignificant; for after the monthly meeting of 1770, I had even withdrawn myself from the militia, by the resignation of an empty and barren commission. My temper is not susceptible of envy, and the view of successful merit has always excited my warmest applause. The miseries of a vacant life were never known to a man whose hours were insufficient of a vacant life were never known to a man whose hours were insufficient for the inexhaustible pleasures of study. But I lamented that at the proper age I had not embraced the lucrative pursuits of the law or of trade, the chances of civil office or India adventure, or even the fat slumbers of the church; and my repentance became more lively as the loss of time was more irretrievable.

From *Memoirs of My Life and Writings*, 1796.

Fanny Burney

He had put the pistol upon a table, and had his hand in his pocket, whence, in a few moments, he took out another: he then emptied something on the table from a small leather bag; after which, taking up both the pistols, one in each hand, he drops hastily upon his knees, and called out, "O God!—forgive me!"

In a moment, strength and courage seemed lent me as by inspiration: I started, and rushing precipitately into the room, just caught his arm, and then, overcome by my own fears, I fell down at his side, breathless and senseless. My recovery, however, was, I believe, almost instantaneous; and then the sight of this unhappy man, regarding me with a look of unutterable astonishment, mixed with concern, presently restored to me my recollection. I arose, though with difficulty; he did the same; the pistols, as I soon saw, were both on the floor.

Unwilling to leave them, and indeed, too weak to move, I lent one hand on the table, and then stood perfectly still: while he, his eyes cast wildly towards me, seemed too infinitely amazed to be capable of either speech or action.

From *Evelina*, 1778.

Mary Wollstonecraft

I may be accused of arrogance; still I must declare what I firmly believe, that all the writers who have written on the subject of female education and manners, from Rousseau to Dr. Gregory, have contributed to render women more artificial, weak characters, than they would otherwise have been and consequently, more useless members of society. I might have expressed this conviction in a lower key, but I am afraid it would have been the whine of affectation, and not the faithful expression of my feelings, of the clear result which experience and reflection have led me to draw. When I come to that

division of the subject, I shall advert to the passages that I more particularly
disapprove of, in the works of the authors I have just alluded to; but it is first
necessary to observe that my objection extends to the whole purport of those
books, which tend, in my opinion, to degrade one-half of the human species,
and render women pleasing at the expense of every solid virtue.

From *Vindication of the Rights of Woman,* 1792

Washington Irving

The dominant spirit, however, that haunts this enchanted region and seems
to be commander-in-chief of all powers of the air, is the apparition of a figure on horseback without a head. It is said by some to be the ghost of a Hes-
sian trooper, whose head had been carried away by a cannon-ball, in some
nameless battle during the revolutionary war; and who is ever and anon seen
by the country folk, hurrying along in the gloom of night, as if on the wings
of the wind. His haunts are not confined to the valley, but extend at times to
the adjacent roads, and especially to the vicinity of a church at no great distance. Indeed, certain of the most authentic historians of those parts, who
have been careful in collecting and collating the floating facts concerning
this spectre, allege that the body of the trooper having been buried in the
churchyard, the ghost rides forth to the scene of battle in nightly quest of his
head; and that the rushing speed with which he sometimes passes along the
Hollow, like a midnight blast, is owing to his being belated and in a hurry to
get back to the churchyard before daybreak.

From "The Legend of Sleepy Hollow," *The Sketch-Book,* 1819–20.

William Hazlitt

Any one may mouth out a passage with a theatrical cadence, or get upon
stilts to tell his thoughts; but to write or speak with propriety and simplicity
is a more difficult task. Thus it is easy to affect a pompous style, to use a
word twice as big as the thing you want to express: it is not so easy to pitch
upon the very word that exactly fits it. Out of eight or ten words equally
common, equally intelligible, with nearly equal pretensions, it is a matter of
some nicety and discrimination to pick out the very one, the preferableness
of which is scarcely perceptible, but decisive. The reason why I object to Dr.
Johnson's style is that there is no discrimination, no selection, no variety in it.
He uses none but "tall, opaque words," taken from the "first row of the
rubric"—words with the greatest number of syllables, or Latin phrases with
merely English terminations. If a fine style depended on this sort of arbitrary
pretension, it would be fair to judge of an author's elegance by the measure-
ment of his words, and the substitution of foreign circumlocutions (with no
precise associations) for the mother-tongue. How simple it is to be dignified
without ease, to be pompous without meaning! Surely, it is but a mechanical
rule for avoiding what is low to be always pedantic and affected. It is clear

you cannot use a vulgar English word, if you never use a common English word at all. A fine tact is shewn in adhering to those which are perfectly common, and yet never falling into any expressions which are debased by disgusting circumstances, or which owe their significance and point to technical or professional allusions. A truly natural or familiar style can never be quaint or vulgar, for this reason, that it is of universal force and applicability, and that quaintness and vulgarity arise out of the immediate connection of certain words with coarse and disagreeable, or with confined, ideas.

From "On Familiar Style," 1821.

Jane Austen

Mr. Bingley had soon made himself acquainted with all the principal people in the room; he was lively and unreserved, danced every dance, was angry that the ball closed so early, and talked of giving one himself at Netherfield. Such amiable qualities must speak for themselves. What a contrast between him and his friend! Mr. Darcy danced only once with Mrs. Hurst and once with Miss Bingley, declined being introduced to any other lady, and spent the rest of the evening in walking about the room, speaking occasionally to one of his own party. His character was decided. He was the proudest, most disagreeable man in the world, and everybody hoped that he would never come there again. Amongst the most violent against him was Mrs. Bennet, whose dislike of his general behavior was sharpened into particular resentment by his having slighted one of her daughters.

From *Pride and Prejudice*, 1813.

Charles Lamb

I am by nature extremely susceptible of street affronts; the jeers and taunts of the populace; the low-bred triumph they display over the casual trip, or splashed stocking, of a gentleman. Yet can I endure the jocularity of a young sweep with something more than forgiveness. In the last winter but one, pacing along Cheapside with my accustomed precipitation when I walk westward, a treacherous slide brought me upon my back in an instant. I scrambled up with pain and shame enough—yet outwardly trying to face it down, as if nothing had happened—when the roguish grin of one of these young wits encountered me. There he stood, pointing me out with his dusky finger to the mob, and to a poor woman (I suppose his mother) in particular, till the tears for the exquisiteness of the fun (so he thought it) worked themselves out at the corners of his poor red eyes, red from many a previous weeping, and soot-inflamed, yet twinkling through all with such a joy, snatched out of desolation that Hogarth—but Hogarth has got him already (how could he miss him?) in "The March to Finchley," grinning at the pieman—there he stood, as he stands in the picture, irremovable, as if the jest was to last for ever—with such a maximum of glee, and minimum of mischief, in his mirth—for the grin of a genuine sweep hath absolutely no malice in it—that I could have been content, if the honour of a gentleman might endure it, to have remained his butt and his mockery till midnight.

From "The Praise of Chimney-Sweepers," 1822.

George Eliot (Mary Ann Cross)

She was naturally the subject of many observations this evening, for the dinner-party was large and rather more miscellaneous as to the male portion than any which had been held at the Grange since Mr. Brooke's nieces had resided with him, so that the talking was done in duos and trios more or less inharmonious. There was the newly-elected mayor of Middlemarch, who happened to be a manufacturer; the philanthropic banker his brother-in-law, who predominated so much in the town that some called him a Methodist, others a hypocrite, according to the resources of their vocabulary; and there were various professional men. In fact, Mrs. Cadwallader said that Brooke was beginning to treat the Middlemarchers, and that she preferred the farmers at the tithe-dinner, who drank her health unpretentiously, and were not ashamed of their grandfathers' furniture. For in that part of the country, before Reform had done its notable part in developing the political consciousness, there was a clearer distinction of ranks and a dimmer distinction of parties; so that Mr. Brooke's miscellaneous invitations seemed to belong to that general laxity which came from his inordinate travel and habit of taking too much in the form of ideas.

From *Middlemarch*, 1871–72.

Abraham Lincoln

Fourscore and seven years ago our fathers brought forth on this continent a new nation, conceived in liberty and dedicated to the proposition that all men are created equal.

Now we are engaged in a great civil war, testing whether that nation, or any nation so conceived and so dedicated, can long endure. We are met on a great battle-field of that war. We have come to dedicate a portion of that field as a final resting-place for those who here gave their lives that that nation might live. It is altogether fitting and proper that we should do this.

But, in a larger sense, we cannot dedicate—we cannot consecrate—we cannot hallow—this ground. The brave men, living and dead, who struggled here, have consecrated it far above our poor power to add or detract. The world will little note nor long remember what we say here, but it can never forget what they did here. It is for us, the living, rather, to be dedicated here to the unfinished work which they who fought here have thus far so nobly advanced. It is rather for us to be here dedicated to the great task remaining before us—that from these honored dead we take increased devotion to that cause for which they gave the last full measure of devotion; that we here highly resolve that these dead shall not have died in vain; that this nation, under God, shall have a new birth of freedom; and that government of the people, by the people, for the people, shall not perish from the earth.

From *The Gettysburg Address*, 1863.

Mark Twain

Once a day a cheap, gaudy packet arrived upward from St. Louis, and another downward from Keokuk. Before these events, the day was glorious with expectancy; after them, the day was a dead and empty thing. Not only the boys, but the whole village, felt this. After all these years I can picture that old time to myself now, just as it was then: the white town drowsing in the sunshine of a summer's morning; the streets empty, or pretty nearly so; one or two clerks sitting in front of the Water Street stores, with their splint-bottomed chairs tilted back against the walls, chins on breasts, hats slouched over their faces, asleep—with shingle-shavings enough around to show what broke them down; a sow and a litter of pigs loafing along the sidewalk, doing a good business in watermelon rinds and seeds; two or three lonely little freight piles scattered about the "levee"; a pile of "skids" on the slope of the stone-paved wharf, and the fragrant town drunkard asleep in the shadow of them; two or three wood flats at the head of the wharf, but nobody to listen to the peaceful lapping of the wavelets against them; the great Mississippi, the majestic, the magnificent Mississippi, rolling its mile-wide tide along, shining in the sun; the dense forest away on the other side; the "point" above the town, and the "point" below, bounding the river-glimpse and turning it into a sort of sea, and withal a very still and brilliant and lonely one. Presently a film of dark smoke appears above one of those remote "points"; instantly a negro drayman, famous for his quick eye and prodigious voice, lifts up the cry, "S-t-e-a-m-boat a-comin'!" and the scene changes! The town drunkard stirs, the clerks wake up, a furious clatter of drays follows, every house and store pours out a human contribution, and all in a twinkling the dead town is alive and moving. Drays, carts, men, boys, all go hurrying from many quarters to a common center, the wharf. Assembled there, the people fasten their eyes upon the coming boat as upon a wonder they are seeing for the first time.

From *Life on the Mississippi*, 1883.

Henry James

The house of fiction has in short not one window, but a million—a number of possible windows not to be reckoned, rather; every one of which has been pierced, or is still pierceable, in its vast front, by the need of the individual vision and by the pressure of the individual will. These apertures, of dissimilar shape and size, hang so, all together, over the human scene that we might have expected of them a greater sameness of report than we find. They are but windows at the best, mere holes in a dead wall, disconnected, perched aloft; they are not hinged doors opening straight upon life. But they have this mark of their own that at each of them stands a figure with a pair of eyes, or at least with a field-glass, with forms, again and again, for observation, a unique instrument, insuring to the person making use of it an impression distinct from every other. He and his neighbours are watching the same show, but one seeing more where the other sees less, one seeing black where the other sees white, one seeing big where the other sees small, one seeing coarse where the other sees fine. And so on, and so on; there is fortunately no saying on what, for the particular pair of eyes, the window may *not* open; "fortunately" by reason, precisely, of this incalculability of range. The spreading field, the human scene, is the "choice of subject"; the pierced aperture, either broad or balconied or slit-like and low-browed, is the "literary form"; but they are, singly or together, as nothing without the posted presence of the watcher—without, in other words, the consciousness of the artist. Tell me what the artist is, and I will tell you of what he has *been* conscious. Thereby I shall express to you at once his boundless freedom and his "moral" reference.

From the Preface to *The Portrait of a Lady,* 1915.

Ernest Hemingway

Sometimes in the dark we heard the troops marching under the window and the guns going past pulled by motor-tractors. There was much traffic at night and many mules on the roads with boxes of ammunition on each side of their packsaddles and gray motor-trucks that carried men, and other trucks with loads covered with canvas that moved slower in the traffic. There were big guns too that passed in the day drawn by tractors, the long barrels of the guns covered with green branches and green leafy branches and vines laid over the tractors. To the north we could look across a valley and see a forest of chestnut trees and behind it another mountain on this side of the river. There was fighting for that mountain too, but it was not successful, and in the fall when the rains came the leaves all fell from the chestnut trees and the branches were bare and the trunks black with rain. The vineyards were thin and bare-branched too and all the country wet and brown and dead with the autumn. There were mists over the river and clouds on the mountain and the trucks splashed mud on the road and the troops were muddy and wet in their capes; their rifles were wet and under their capes the two leather cartridge-boxes on the front of the belts, gray leather boxes heavy with the packs of clips of thin, long 6.5 mm. cartridges, bulged forward under the capes so that the men, passing on the road, marched as though they were six months gone with child.

Jean Shepherd

When we got the ham home, my mother immediately stripped off the white paper and the string in the middle of our chipped white-enamel kitchen table. There it lay, exuding heavenly perfumes—proud, arrogant, regal. It had a dark, smoked, leathery skin, which my mother carefully peeled off with her sharpened bread knife. Then the old man, the only one who could lift the ham without straining a gut, placed it in the big dark-blue oval pot that was used only for hams. My mother then covered the ham with water, pushed it onto the big burner and turned up the gas until it boiled. It just sat there on the stove and bubbled away for maybe two hours, filling the house with a smell that was so luscious, so powerful as to have erotic overtones. The old man paced back and forth, occasionally lifting the lid and prodding the ham with a fork, inhaling deeply. The ham frenzy was upon him.

N. Scott Momaday

Although my grandmother lived out her long life in the shadow of Rainy Mountain, the immense landscape of the continental interior lay like memory in her blood. She could tell of the Crows, whom she had never seen, and of the Black Hills, where she had never been. I wanted to see in reality what she had seen more perfectly in the mind's eye, and travelled fifteen hundred miles to begin my pilgrimage.

Yellowstone, it seemed to me, was the top of the world, a region of deep lakes and dark timber, canyons and waterfalls. But, beautiful as it is, one might have the sense of confinement there. The skyline in all directions is close at hand, the high wall of the woods and deep cleavages of shade. There is a perfect freedom in the mountains, but it belongs to the eagle and the elk, the badger and the bear. The Kiowas reckoned their stature by the distance they could see, and they were bent and blind in the wilderness.

E. B. White

I had marked Apathy's hatching date on my desk calendar. On the night before the goslings were due to arrive, when I made my rounds before going to bed, I looked in on her. She hissed, as usual, and ran her neck out. When I shone my light at her, two tiny green heads were visible, thrusting their way through her feathers. The goslings were here—a few hours ahead of schedule. My heart leapt up. Outside, in the barnyard, both ganders stood vigil.

They knew very well what was up: ganders take an enormous interest in family affairs and are deeply impressed by the miracle of the egg-that-becomes-goose. I shut the door against them and went to bed.

From E. B. White, "Geese." In *Essays of E. B. White*. New York: Harper & Row, 1971. Reprinted by permission of Harper & Row.

James Baldwin

Negroes want to be treated like men: a perfectly straightforward statement, containing only seven words. People who have mastered Kant, Hegel, Shakespeare, Marx, Freud, and the Bible find this statement merely impenetrable. The idea seems to threaten profound, barely conscious assumptions. A kind of panic paralyzes their features, as though they found themselves trapped on the edge of a steep place. I once tried to describe to a very well-known American intellectual the conditions among Negroes in the South. My recital disturbed him and made him indignant; and he asked me in perfect innocence, "Why don't all the Negroes in the South move North?" I tried to explain what *has* happened, unfailingly, whenever a significant body of Negroes move North. They do not escape Jim Crow: they merely encounter another, not-less-deadly variety. They do not move to Chicago, they move to the South Side; they do not move to New York, they move to Harlem. The pressure within the ghetto causes the ghetto walls to expand, and this expansion is always violent. White people hold the line as long as they can, and in as many ways as they can, from verbal intimidation to physical violence. But inevitably the border which has divided the ghetto from the rest of the world falls back bitterly before the black horde; the landlords make a tidy profit by raising the rent, chopping up the rooms, and all but dispensing with the upkeep; and what has once been a neighborhood turns into a "turf." This is precisely what happened when the Puerto Ricans arrived in their thousands—and the bitterness that caused is, as I write, being fought out all up and down those streets.

From James Baldwin, "Fifth Avenue Uptown: A Letter from Harlem," in *Nobody Knows My Name*. Copyright © 1960, 1961 by James Baldwin. Reprinted by permission of The Dial Press, Inc. and Michael Joseph Ltd.

Susan Sontag

This is why so many of the objects prized by Camp taste are old-fashioned, out-of-date, *démodé*. It's not a love of the old as such. It's simply that the process of aging or deterioration provides the necessary detachments—or arouses a necessary sympathy. When the theme is important, and contemporary, the failure of a work of art may make us indignant. Time can change that. Time liberates the work of art from moral relevance, delivering it over to the Camp sensibility. . . . Another effect: time contracts the sphere of banality. (Banality is, strictly speaking, always a category of the contemporary.) What was banal can, with the passage of time, become fantastic. Many people who listen with delight to the style of Rudy Vallee revived by the English pop group The Temperance Seven, would have been driven up the wall by Rudy Vallee in his heyday.

Thus, things are campy, not when they become old—but when we become less involved in them, and can enjoy, instead of be frustrated by, the failure of the attempt. But the effect of time is unpredictable. Maybe "Method" Acting (James Dean, Rod Steiger, Warren Beatty) will seem as Camp some day as Ruby Keeler's does now—or as Sarah Bernhardt's does in the films she made at the end of her career. And maybe not.

Tom Wolfe

The first good look I had at customized cars was at an event called a "Teen Fair," held in Burbank, a suburb of Los Angeles beyond Hollywood. This was a wild place to be taking a look at art objects—eventually, I should say, you have to reach the conclusion that these customized cars *are* art objects, at least if you use the standards applied in a civilized society. But I will get to that in a moment. Anyway, about noon you drive up to a place that looks like an outdoor amusement park, and there are three serious-looking kids, like the cafeteria committee in high school, taking tickets, but the scene inside is quite mad. Inside, two things hit you. The first is a huge platform a good seven feet off the ground with a hully-gully band—everything is electrified, the bass, the guitars, the saxophones—and then behind the band, on the platform, about two hundred kids are doing fantastic dances called the hully-gully, the bird, and the shampoo. As I said, it's noontime. The dances the kids are doing are very jerky. The boys and girls don't touch, not even with their hands. They just ricochet around. Then you notice that all the girls are dressed exactly alike. They have bouffant hairdos—all of them—and slacks that are, well, skin-tight does not get the idea across; it's more the conformation than how tight the slacks are. It's as if some lecherous old tailor with a gluteous-maximus fixation designed them, striation by striation. About the time you've managed to focus on this, you notice that out in the middle of the park is a huge, perfectly round swimming pool; really rather enormous. And there is a Chris-Craft cabin cruiser in the pool, going around and around, sending up big waves, with more of these bouffant babies bunched in the back of it. In the water, suspended like plankton, are kids in Skuba-diving outfits; others are tooling around underwater, breathing through a snorkel. And all over the place are booths, put up by shoe companies and guitar companies and God knows who else, and there are kids dancing in all of them—dancing the bird, the hully-gully, and the shampoo—with the music of the hully-gully band piped all over the park through loudspeakers.

James Dickey

(The man described in these paragraphs has just been shot through the breast with an arrow)

I got up with the gun and the powder, wrapping the string around my right hand. I swung the barrel back and forth to cover everything, the woods and the world. There was nothing in the clearing but Bobby and the shot man and me. Bobby was still on the ground, though now he was lifting his head. I could understand that much, but something kept blurring the clear idea of Bobby and myself and the leaves and the river. The shot man was still standing. He wouldn't concentrate in my vision; I couldn't believe him. He was like a film over the scene, gray and vague, with the force gone out of him; I was amazed at how he did everything. He touched the arrow experimentally, and I could tell that it was set in him as solidly as his breastbone. It was in him tight and unwobbling, coming out front and back. He took hold of it with both hands, but compared to the arrow's strength his hands were weak; they weakened more as I looked, and began to melt. He was on his knees, and then fell to his side, pulling his legs up. He rolled back and forth like a man with the wind knocked out of him, all the time making a bubbling, gritting sound. His lips turned red, but from his convulsions—in which there was something comical and unspeakable—he seemed to gain strength. He got up on one knee and then to his feet again while I stood with the shotgun at port arms. He took a couple of strides toward the woods and then seemed to change his mind and danced back to me, lurching and clog-stepping in a secret circle. He held out a hand to me, like a prophet, and I pointed the shotgun straight at the head of the arrow, ice coming into my teeth. I was ready to put it all behind me with one act, with one pull of a string.

But there was no need. He crouched and fell forward with his face on my white tennis shoe tops, trembled away into his legs and shook down to stillness. He opened his mouth and it was full of blood like an apple. A clear bubble formed on his lips and stayed there.

Barbara Tuchman

In the excitement at St. Paul's the matter of Wyclif had not been tested. The English prelates, caught between clerical interest and national sentiment, might have been content to let the matter drop, but the papacy was not. In May, Gregory XI issued five Bulls addressed to the English episcopacy and to the king and the University of Oxford, condemning Wyclif's errors and demanding his arrest. All discussion of his heretical doctrines was to be suppressed and all who supported them removed from office. An issue full of danger was added to all the other sources of strife. The new Parliament was strongly anti-papal; the king, babbling of hawks and hunting instead of attending to the urgent needs of his soul, was dying. For the moment, while England waited uneasily for the change of reign, the bishops held the proceedings against Wyclif in abeyance.

> From Barbara Tuchman, *A Distant Mirror: The Calamitous 14th Century*. New York: Alfred A. Knopf, 1978. Reprinted by permission of the publisher.

Frances Fitzgerald

After 1900, a new distinction appears in American history textbooks: there are "we Americans," and there are "the immigrants." The textbook discovery of "the immigrants" was actually somewhat belated, since the great wave of European immigration to the United States had been under way for some time. European—and particularly Irish and Germans—had been crossing the Atlantic in large numbers since the eighteen-forties, but between 1881 and 1890 more than five million immigrants came to the United States, and by 1910 the total had risen to more than sixteen million. The newcomers not only increased the American population significantly but altered its ethnic composition. After 1900, immigrants from the southern and eastern countries of Europe vastly outnumbered those from the northern and western ones. The schools were primarily affected, since they were the only public agencies that offered special services for the immigrants. Having been charged with the "Americanization" of the newcomers, they naturally had to take on the task of defining what "an American" was and was not.

> From Frances FitzGerald, *America Revised: History Schoolbooks in the Twentieth Century*. Copyright © 1979 by Frances FitzGerald. Reprinted by permission of Little, Brown and Company.

Alice Walker

Corrine's mother was a dedicated housewife and mother who disliked her more adventurous sister. But she never prevented Corrine from visiting. And when Corrine was old enough, she sent her to Spelman Seminary where Aunt Theodosia had gone. This was a very interesting place. It was started by two white missionaries from New England who used to wear identical dresses. Started in a church basement, it soon moved up to Army barracks. Eventually these two ladies were able to get large sums of money from some of the richest men in America, and so the place grew. Buildings and trees. Girls were taught everything: Reading, Writing, Arithmetic, sewing, cleaning, cooking. But more than anything else, they were taught to serve God and the colored community. Their official motto was OUR WHOLE SCHOOL FOR CHRIST. But I always thought their unofficial motto should have been OUR COMMUNITY COVERS THE WORLD, because no sooner had a young woman got through Spelman Seminary than she began to put her hand to whatever work she could do for her people, anywhere in the world. It was truly astonishing. These very polite and proper young women, some of them never having set foot outside their own small country towns, except to come to the Seminary, thought nothing of packing up for India, Africa, the Orient. Or for Philadelphia or New York.

Richard Rodriquez

It saddened my mother to learn about Mexican-American parents who wanted their children to start working after finishing high school. In schooling she recognized the key to job advancement. And she remembered her past. As a girl, new to America, she had been awarded a diploma by high school teachers too busy or careless to notice that she hardly spoke English. On her own she determined to learn to type. That skill got her clean office jobs and encouraged an optimism about the possibility of advancement. (Each morning when her sisters put on uniforms for work, she chose a bright-colored dress.) She became an excellent speller—of words she mispronounced. ("And I've never been to college," she would say smiling when her children asked about a word they didn't want to look up in a dictionary.)

Joan Didion

It is time for the baby's birthday party: a white cake, strawberry-marshmallow ice cream, a bottle of champagne saved from another party. In the evening, after she has gone to sleep, I kneel beside the crib and touch her face, where it is pressed against the slats, with mine. She is an open and trusting child, unprepared for and unaccustomed to the ambushes of family life, and perhaps it is just as well that I can offer her little of that life. I would like to give her more. I would like to promise her that she will grow up with a sense of her cousins and of rivers and of her great-grandmother's teacups, would like to pledge her a picnic on a river with friend chicken and her hair uncombed, would like to give her *home* for her birthday, but we live differently now and I can promise her nothing like that. I give her a xylophone and a sundress from Madeira, and promise to tell her a funny story.

Shirley Brice Heath

The environment of both boy and girl babies during their first year of life is a very human one. They sleep with family members, are held, carried, and cuddled by family members, and by all residents of the community as well. For all community members of Trackton, not only older brothers and sisters, babies are playthings. When they cry, they are fed, tended, held, and fondled by anyone nearby. Since bottle-feeding is the norm, anyone can take on feeding responsibilities. Babies are restrained from exploring beyond the human interactions which surround them. They have little occasion to coo and babble by themselves or in quiet situations where their babbling sounds can be heard above the general talk which seems to go on around them most of the time. They sleep and eat at will; they are fed when they seem hungry if food is available, and they go to sleep whenever or wherever they become sleepy. They are often walked up to be played with when children come home from school or a visitor comes in, and they are often awake late into the night in the living room where a television or record player blares, or loud conversation is going on. Their inclusion as part of the family is continuous. If they fall asleep in the midst of a lively story-telling session or a family argument, they continue to be held until the person holding them needs to move about. Then someone else takes over. The child is almost never alone and very rarely in the company of only one other person.

Garrison Keillor

School started the day after Labor Day, Tuesday, the Tuesday when my grandfather went, and in 1918 my father, and in 1948 me. It was the same day, in the same brick schoolhouse, the former New Albion Academy, now named Nelson school. The same misty painting of George Washington looked down on us all from above the blackboard, next to his closest friend, Abraham Lincoln. Lincoln was kind and patient, and we looked to him for sympathy. Washington looked as if he had a headache. His mouth was set in a prim pained expression of disapproval. Maybe people made fun of him for his long frizzy hair, which resembled our teacher's, Mrs. Meiers', and that had soured his disposition. She said he had bad teeth—a good lesson for us to remember: to brush after every meal, up and down, thirty times. The great men held the room in their gaze, even the back corner by the windows.

I bent over my desk, trying to make fat vowels sit on the line like fruit, the tails of consonants hang below, and colored maps of English and French empires, and memorized arithmetic tables and state capitals and major exports of many lands, and when I was stumped, looked up to see George Washington's sour look and Lincoln's pity and friendship, an old married couple on the wall. School, their old home, smelled of powerful floor wax and disinfectant, the smell of patriotism.

Toni Morrison

All forty-six men woke to a rifle shot. All forty-six. Three whitemen walked along the trench unlocking the doors one by one. No one stepped through. When the last lock was opened, the three returned and lifted the bars, one by one. And one by one the blackmen emerged—promptly and without the poke of a rifle butt if they had been there more than a day; promptly with the butt if, like Paul D, they had just arrived. When all forty-six were standing in a line in the trench, another rifle shot signaled the climb out and up to the ground above, where one thousand feet of the best hand-forged chain in Georgia stretched. Each man bent and waited. The first man picked up the end and threaded it through the loop in his leg iron. He stood up then, and, shuffling a little, brought the chain tip to the next prisoner, who did likewise. As the chain was passed on and each man stood in the other's place, the line of men turned around, facing the boxes they had come out of. Not one spoke to the other. At least not with words. The eyes had to tell what there was to tell: "Help me this morning; 's bad"; "I'm a make it"; "New man"; "Steady now steady."

Eudora Welty

She's not the only teacher who has influenced me, but Miss Duling, in some fictional shape or form, has stridden into a larger part of my work than I'd realized until now. She emerges in my perhaps inordinate number of schoolteacher characters. I loved those characters in the writing. But I did not, in life, love Miss Duling. I was afraid of her high-arched bony nose, her eyebrows lifted in half-circles above her hooded, brilliant eyes, and of the Kentucky R's in her speech, and the long steps she took in her hightop shoes. I did nothing but fear her bearing-down authority, and did not connect this (as of course we were meant to) with our own need or desire to learn, perhaps because I already had this wish, and did not need to be driven.

Imitating Sentence Patterns

After you have spent some time merely copying passages, you might attempt another kind of imitation. You can take individual sentences as patterns on which to devise sentences of your own. This is a more difficult exercise than the verbatim copying, but it pays high dividends to those who use it conscientiously.

How closely should you follow the model? As closely as you care to, is the most sensible answer. But you will find this exercise most fruitful if you will observe at least the same *kind, number*, and *order* of clauses and phrases. If the model sentence has an adverb clause, you should write an adverb clause. If the model sentence is introduced by a participial phrase, you should put a participial phrase in the lead-off position. If the model sentence has three noun clauses arranged in parallel structure, you should write a sentence containing three noun clauses in a similar structure.

The aim of this exercise is not to achieve a word-for-word correspondence with the model but rather to achieve an awareness of the variety of sentence structures of which the English language is capable. The reason why many students never venture outside their puerile, monotonous sentence structure is that they have never attempted sophisticated sentence patterns. Writing such patterns according to models will increase their syntactical resources. And with more resources at their command, they will acquire more confidence in their writing ability.

No one, of course, says while he or she is writing, "I just wrote a compound sentence interspersed with gerund phrases. This time I think I'll begin my sentence with an adverb clause and use a series of noun clauses as the object of the main verb." Such a self-conscious approach to writing would undoubtedly result in some monstrous prose.

No, our prose must come as naturally as—to use Keats's words—"the leaves to the trees." The kind of prose we write cannot be arbitrary; it is governed by the subject matter, the occasion, the purpose, the audience, and the personality of the writer. If it is true that matter and form are intimately related, then there must be one best way in which to say a particular thing for a given audience and purpose. But as a practical matter, what we manage to achieve most of the time is one of a number of *better* ways to say something. Coleridge once said that the infallible test of a perfect style was "its *untranslatableness* in words of the same language without injury to the meaning." Only seldom, perhaps, do we achieve this kind of "inevitable prose." What we achieve most of the time is, at best, an adequate prose.

A great deal of the writing you may be called upon to do in the future will be impromptu, spur-of-the-moment writing. While you are still in school, you will have to write essay-type examinations, where you have little time for reflection and almost no time for revision. In your job someday, you will have to dash off memos, directives, and letters. As a private citizen, you will have to scribble off notes to send to school with your children, pen a hurried letter to your parents, pound out a letter to the editor of the local newspaper. The more practice you have had in writing, the better will be this one-draft prose.

But you may also be called upon at times to do some writing that entails a great deal of reflection, research, organization, and revision. You may have to write a report to be read to the board of governors or prepare a speech to be delivered before the Chamber of Commerce. It is this kind of deliberate writing that will call upon all the inventive and stylistic resources at your command. This will necessarily be slow writing, but it does not have to be labored writing for being slow. Someone once said that "hard writing makes for easy reading." And Quintilian once said, "Write quickly and you will never write well; write well and you will soon write quickly."

So with these cautions and objectives in mind, now try your hand at imitating the sentence patterns of practiced writers. You may never in your life have occasion to write a sentence like some of those that you have mechanically imitated in this exercise, but you will be none the worse for having gone through the paces.

As examples of how to imitate sentence patterns, a few samples of the method are printed below. For models, you can select sentences from your favorite authors, or you can use sentences from the specimen passages reproduced in this chapter.

Sample Imitations

MODEL SENTENCE: The gallows stood in a small yard, separate from the main grounds of the prison and overgrown with tall prickly weeds.—George Orwell, *Burmese Days*

(Write a sentence according to the pattern of the model sentence.)

IMITATION: The dog shivered in the background, wet from nosing his way through the early-morning grasses and covered with damp cockle-spurs.

MODEL SENTENCE: He went through the narrow alley of Temple Bar quickly, muttering to himself that they could all go to hell because he was going to have a good night of it.—James Joyce, "Counterparts"

IMITATION: They stood outside on the wet pavement of the terrace, pretending that they had not heard us when we called to them from the library.

MODEL SENTENCE: To regain the stage in its own character, not as a mere emulation of prose, poetry must find its own poetic way to the mastery the stage demands—the mastery of action. Archibald MacLeish, "The Poet as Playwright"

IMITATION: To discover our own natures, not the personalities imposed on us by others, we must honestly assess the values we cherish—in short, our "philosophy of life."

MODEL SENTENCE: If one must worship a bully, it is better that he should be a policeman than a gangster.—George Orwell, "Raffles and Miss Blandish"

IMITATION: Since he continued to be belligerent, it was plain that cajoling would prove more effective than scolding.

MODEL SENTENCE: I went to the woods because I wished to live deliberately, to front only the essential facts of life, and see if I could learn what it had to teach, and not, when I came to die, discover that I had not lived.—Henry David Thoreau, *Walden*

IMITATION: I greeted him politely, although I planned to challenge him repeatedly, to assess his erudition, to test whether he could discriminate what was expedient in each situation, and, after I had probed him thoroughly, to announce that we had no place for him in our organization.

MODEL SENTENCE: To have even a portion of this illuminated reason and true philosophy is the highest state to which nature can aspire, in the way of intellect.—John Henry Newman, *The Idea of a University*

IMITATION: To win a measure of his affection and esteem was the most difficult task that I had ever assigned myself.

MODEL SENTENCE: As most of these old Custom House officers had good traits and as my position in reference to them, being paternal and protective, was favorable to the growth of friendly sentiments, I soon grew to like them all.—Nathaniel Hawthorne, *Scarlet Letter*

IMITATION: When he offered me the gift and when his classmates, perceiving his embarrassment, discreetly withheld their applause, I gratefully accepted his gesture of friendship.

MODEL SENTENCE: The real art that dealt with life directly was that of the first men who told their stories round the savage camp-fire.—Robert Louis Stevenson, "A Humble Remonstrance"

IMITATION: The man who insists on perfection in others is the man who is most tolerant of imperfection in himself.

MODEL SENTENCE: The most important Indian grouping on the continent, north of Mexico, from the very beginning of European conquest on through and after the American Revolution was the Confederacy of the Iroquois.—John Collier, *Indians of the Americas*

IMITATION: The foremost alliance in Europe, amenable to expansion, during the eighteenth century and again after the collapse of the three-nation concordant, was the pact among the Big Four.

MODEL SENTENCE: This brings us to that growing army of "publicity men" and women who sometimes do not—but frequently do—give the best of their years and their vitality to pushing causes in which they have no faith and to becoming personalities whom privately they designated as stuffed shirts.—Stuart Chase, "The Luxury of Integrity"

IMITATION: He presented a startling conglomeration of statistics and testimonies that confirmed—or allegedly confirmed—the general's capacity for subverting causes of which he was suspicious and toward minimizing faults that he considered "politically innocent."

Another exercise that can be worked off this concentration on a single sentence is to vary the pattern of the model sentence or to devise an alternate way of expressing it. At the beginning of this section on imitation, we mentioned the 150 variations that Erasmus worked off a single Latin sentence. Besides making you aware that style is the result of choices that a writer makes from among the available lexical and syntactical resources, such an exercise forces you to discover the options that are available to you. Varying the sentence pattern usually calls for nothing more than a reordering of the words in the original sentence. Devising an alternate expression, however, often involves the choice of different words and different syntactical structures. Let us take the first three model sentences that we worked with earlier and show how they might be varied and altered.

MODEL SENTENCE: The gallows stood in a small yard, separate from the main grounds and overgrown with tall prickly weeds.—George Orwell, *Burmese Days*

VARIATION OF THE PATTERN: In a small yard, separate from the main grounds and overgrown with tall prickly weeds, stood the gallows.

ALTERNATE EXPRESSIONS: Located in a small yard, which was overgrown with tall prickly weeds, the gallows was separated from the main grounds.

The gallows was situated outside the main grounds, in a small yard that was overgrown with tall prickly weeds.

(Transformational grammar can be a help in suggesting alternate ways of phrasing a sentence. Reducing the model sentence to its "kernel sentences" can reveal how the "deep structure" was transformed into the "surface structure" that the author actually wrote. These are some of the "kernel sentences" of Orwell's sentence:

The gallows stood in a yard.
The yard was small.
The yard was separate from the main grounds.
Or: The gallows was separate from the main grounds.
The yard was overgrown with weeds.

Or: The gallows was overgrown with weeds.
The weeds were tall.
The weeds were prickly.

There is some ambiguity of structure in the Orwell sentence, because the two adjectival phrases "separate from . . ." and "overgrown with . . ." could modify *gallows* or *yard*. By reducing the original sentence to its kernels, however, you can see how Orwell transformed them into different grammatical combinations and can see what other combinations are possible.)

MODEL SENTENCE: He went through the narrow alley of Temple Bar quickly, muttering to himself that they could all go to hell because he was going to have a good night of it.—James Joyce, "Counterparts"

VARIATION OF THE PATTERN: Muttering to himself that they could all to go hell because he was going to have a good night of it, he went quickly through the narrow alley of Temple Bar.

ALTERNATE EXPRESSIONS: As he went quickly through the narrow alley of Temple Bar, he muttered to himself that they could all go to hell, for he was going to have a good night of it.

"You can all go to hell," he muttered to himself as he went quickly through the narrow alley of Temple Bar. "I am going to have a good night of it."

MODEL SENTENCE: To regain the stage in its own character, not as a mere emulation of prose, poetry must find its own poetic way to the mastery the stage demands—the mastery of action.—Archibald MacLeish, "The Poet as Playwright"

VARIATION OF THE PATTERN: Poetry must find its own poetic way to the mastery the stage demands—the mastery of action—if it is to regain the stage in its own character, not as a mere emulator of prose.

ALTERNATE EXPRESSIONS: Poetry can regain the stage in its own character, not as a mere emulator of prose, only if it can master the kind of action that the stage peculiarly demands.

If poetry is to regain the stage in its own character, it must master the kind of action that the stage peculiarly demands; otherwise it will remain a mere emulator of prose.

All of these exercises in imitation—copying passages, writing original sentences according to pattern, varying the pattern of a model sentence, and devising alternate expressions for the same thought—can teach you a number of valuable lessons: (1) they can make you aware of the variety of lexical and syntactical resources which your language offers; (2) they can afford you practice in choosing apt words and collocating them in various ways; (3) they can teach you that not every variation is equally clear, graceful, or appropriate; (4) they can teach you that variation of the pattern of the sentence often results in a different *effect* and that an alternate expression often results in a different *meaning*. The ultimate goal of all imitation exercises, however, is eventually to cut you loose from your models, equipped with the competence and resources to go it on your own.

Readings

Hugh Blair: Critical Examination of the Style of Mr. Addison in No. 411 of "The Spectator"*

In 1759, Dr. Hugh Blair began teaching rhetoric at the University of Edinburgh, and in 1762, he was appointed the first Regius Professor of Rhetoric and Belles Lettres at Edinburgh. In 1783, upon his retirement from this post, Blair published the forty-seven lectures on rhetoric and literature that he had presented for twenty-four years to packed classrooms. This text Lectures on Rhetoric and Belles Lettres *became a widely used book in the English and American schools in the late eighteenth and early nineteenth century.*

Midway in the course of lectures Blair presented detailed stylistic analyses of four of Addison's Spectator *essays (Nos. 411–14) and an analysis of Jonathan Swift's "A Proposal for Correcting, Improving, and Ascertaining the English Tongue." These analyses represent one of the few instances in English of a stylistic analysis of an entire essay.*

Blair comments on points of grammar, usage, and style in Addison's essays. From the reprinting of Blair's first analysis, students will learn one technique of analyzing, pointedly and concretely, English prose sentences and may become more conscious of their own prose style. Some of Blair's strictures on Addison's style, such as his views on the relative pronouns which *and* that, *are delivered from the standpoint of eighteenth-century usage. And while some of Blair's comments may strike a modern audience as being somewhat picky, most students will find Blair's criticism judicious. In almost every case where Blair has rewritten Addison's sentences, students will notice an improvement in the neatness and clarity of the prose.*

Occasionally, Blair's style of punctuation has been silently changed.

I have insisted fully on the subject of language and style, both because it is, in itself, of great importance and because it is more capable of being ascertained by precise rule, than several other parts of composition. A critical analysis of the style of some good author will tend further to illustrate the subject, as it will suggest observations which I have not had occasion to make and will show, in the most practical light, the use of those which I have made.

*Lecture XX of Blair's *Lectures on Rhetoric and Belles Lettres*, first published in 1783.

Mr. Addison is the author whom I have chosen for this purpose. *The Spectator*, of which his papers are the chief ornament, is a book which is in the hands of every one and which cannot be praised too highly. The good sense and good writing, the useful morality and the admirable vein of humour which abound in it, render it one of those standard books which have done the greatest honour to the English nation. I have formerly given the general character of Mr. Addison's style and manner as natural and unaffected, easy and polite, and full of those graces which a flowery imagination diffuses over writing. At the same time, though one of the most beautiful writers in the language, he is not the most correct; a circumstance which renders his composition the more proper to be the subject of our present criticism. The free and flowing manner of this amiable writer sometimes led him into inaccuracies which the more studied circumspection and care of far inferior writers have taught them to avoid. Remarking his beauties, therefore, which I shall have frequent occasion to do, as I proceed, I must also point out his negligences and defects. Without a free, impartial discussion, of both the faults and beauties which occur in his composition, it is evident this piece of criticism would be of no service; and from the freedom which I use in criticising Mr. Addison's style, none can imagine that I mean to depreciate his writings, after having repeatedly declared the high opinion which I entertain of them. The beauties of this author are so many and the general character of his style is so elegant and estimable that the minute imperfections I shall have occasion to point out are but like those spots in the sun, which may be discovered by the assistance of art but which have no effect in obscuring its lustre. It is, indeed, my judgment that what Quintilian applies to Cicero, "*Ille se profecisse sciat, cui Cicero valde placebit,*" may, with justice, be applied to Mr. Addison: that to be highly pleased with his manner of writing is the criterion of one's having acquired a good taste in English style. The paper on which we are now to enter is No. 411, the first of his celebrated Essays on the Pleasures of the Imagination in the sixth volume of *The Spectator*. It begins thus:

(1) Our sight is the most perfect and most delightful of all our senses.

This is an excellent introductory sentence. It is clear, precise, and simple. The author lays down, in a few plain words, the proposition which he is going to illustrate throughout the rest of the paragraph. In this manner, we should always set out. A first sentence should seldom be a long, and never an intricate, one.

He might have said, "*Our sight is the most perfect and the most delightful.*" But he has judged better in omitting to repeat the article *the*. For the repetition of it is proper, chiefly when we intend to point out the objects of which we speak, as distinguished from, or contrasted with, each other; and when we want that the reader's attention should rest on that distinction. For instance, had Mr. Addison intended to say that our sight is at once the most *delightful* and the most *useful* of all our senses, the article might then have been repeated with propriety, as a clear and strong distinction would have been conveyed. But as between *perfect* and *delightful* there is less contrast, there was no occasion for such repetition. It would have had no other effect but to add a word unnecessarily to the sentence. He proceeds:

> (2) It fills the mind with the largest variety of ideas, converses with its objects at the greatest distance, and continues the longest in action, without out being tired or satiated with its proper enjoyments.

This sentence deserves attention, as remarkably harmonious and well constructed. It possesses, indeed, almost all the properties of a perfect sentence. It is entirely perspicuous. It is loaded with no superfluous or unnecessary words. For *tired or satiated* towards the end of the sentence are not used for synonymous terms. They convey distinct ideas and refer to different members of the period: that this sense *continues the longest in action without being tired,* that is, without being fatigued with its action; and also, without being *satiated with its proper enjoyments.* That quality of a good sentence which I termed its unity is here perfectly preserved. It is *our sight* of which he speaks. This is the object carried through the sentence and presented to us, in every member of it, by those verbs, *fills, converses, continues,* to each of which it is clearly the nominative. Those capital words are disposed of in the most proper places; and that uniformity is maintained in the construction of the sentence which suits the unity of the object.

Observe, too, the music of the period; consisting of three members, each of which, agreeable to a rule I formerly mentioned, grows and rises above the other in sound, till the sentence is conducted, at last, to one of the most melodious closes which our language admits—*without being tired or satiated with its proper enjoyments. Enjoyments* is a word of length and dignity, exceedingly proper for a close which is designed to be a musical one. The harmony is the more happy, as this disposition of the members of the period which suits the sound so well is no less just and proper with respect to the sense. It follows the order of nature. First, we have the variety of objects mentioned, which sight furnishes to the mind; next, we have the action of sight on those objects; and lastly, we have the time and continuance of its action. No order could be more natural and happy.

This sentence has still another beauty. It is figurative, without being too much so for the subject. A metaphor runs through it. The sense of sight is, in some degree, personified. We are told of its *conversing* with its objects; and of its not being *tired or satiated* with its *enjoyments;* all which expressions are plain allusions to the actions and feelings of men. This is that slight sort of personification which, without any appearance of boldness and without elevating the fancy much above its ordinary state, renders discourse picturesque and leads us to conceive the author's meaning more distinctly, by clothing abstract ideas, in some degree, with sensible colours. Mr. Addison abounds with this beauty of style beyond most authors; and the sentence which we have been considering is very expressive of his manner of writing.

There is no blemish in it whatever, unless that a strict critic might perhaps object that the epithet *large,* which he applies to *variety—the largest variety of ideas*—is an epithet more commonly applied to extent than to number. It is plain that he here employed it to avoid the repetition of the word *great,* which occurs immediately afterwards.

> (3) The sense of feeling can, indeed, give us a notion of extension, shape, and all other ideas that enter at the eye, except colours; but, at the same time, it is very much straitened and confined in its operations to the number, bulk, and distance of its particular objects.

This sentence is by no means so happy as the former. It is, indeed, neither clear nor elegant. *Extension* and *shape* can, with no propriety, be called *ideas;* they are properties of matter. Neither is it accurate, even according to Mr. Locke's philosophy (with which our author seems here to have puzzled himself), to speak of any sense *giving us a notion of ideas;* our senses give us the ideas themselves. The meaning would have been much more clear if the author had expressed himself thus: "The sense of feeling can, indeed, give us the idea of extension, figure, and all the other properties of matter which are perceived by the eye, except colours."

The latter part of the sentence is still more embarrassed. For what meaning can we make of the sense of feeling being *confined in its operation to the number, bulk, and distance, of its particular objects?* Surely, every sense is confined, as much as the sense of feeling, to the number, bulk, and distance of its own objects. Sight and feeling are, in this respect, perfectly on a level; neither of them can extend beyond its own objects. The turn of expression is so inaccurate here that one would be apt to suspect two words to have been omitted in the printing, which were originally in Mr. Addison's manuscript, because the insertion of them would render the sense much more intelligible and clear. These two words are *with regard—it is very much straitened and confined in its operations, with regard to the number, bulk, and distance of its particular objects.* The meaning then would be that feeling is more limited than sight *in this respect*—that it is confined to a narrower circle, to a smaller number of objects.

The epithet *particular,* applied to *objects,* in the conclusion of the sentence, is redundant and conveys no meaning whatever. Mr. Addison seems to have used it in place of *peculiar,* as indeed he does often in other passages of his writings. But *particular* and *peculiar,* though they are too often confounded, are words of different import from each other. *Particular* stands opposed to *general; peculiar* stands opposed to what is possessed in *common with others. Particular* expresses what, in the logical style, is called *species; peculiar,* what is called *differentia. Its peculiar objects* would have signified, in this place, the objects of the sense of feeling, as distinguished from the objects of any other sense and would have had more meaning than *its particular objects,* though, in truth, neither the one nor the other epithet was requisite. It was sufficient to have said simply, *its objects.*

> (4) Our sight seems designed to supply all these defects, and may be considered as a more delicate and diffusive kind of touch, that spreads itself over an infinite multitude of bodies, comprehends the largest figures, and brings into our reach some of the most remote parts of the universe.

Here again the author's style returns upon us in all its beauty. This is a sentence distinct, graceful, well arranged, and highly musical. In the latter part of it, it is constructed with three members, which are formed much in the same manner with those of the second sentence, on which I bestowed so much praise. The construction is so similar that if it had followed immediately after it, we should have been sensible of a faulty monotony. But the interposition of another sentence between them prevents this effect.

> (5) It is this sense which furnishes the imagination with its ideas; so that by the pleasures of the imagination or fancy (which I shall use promiscuously) I here mean such as arise from visible objects, either when we have them actually in our view or when we call up their ideas into our minds by paintings, statues, descriptions, or any the like occasion.

In place of, *It is this sense which furnishes,* the author might have said more shortly, *This sense furnishes.* But the mode of expression which he has used is here more proper. This sort of full and ample assertion, *it is this which,* is fit to be used when a proposition of importance is laid down to which we seek to call the reader's attention. It is like pointing with the hand at the object of which we speak. The parenthesis in the middle of the sentence, *which I shall use promiscuously,* is not clear. He ought to have said, *terms which I shall use promiscuously;* as the verb *use* relates not to the pleasures of the imagination but to the terms of fancy and imagination, which he was to employ as synonymous. *Any the like occasion.* To call a painting or a statue *an occasion* is not a happy expression, nor is it very proper to speak of *calling up ideas by occasions.* The common phrase, *any such means,* would have been more natural.

> (6) We cannot indeed have a single image in the fancy that did not make its first entrance through the sight; but we have the power of retaining, altering, and compounding those images which we have once received into all the varieties of picture and vision that are most agreeable to the imagination; for, by this faculty, a man in a dungeon is capable of entertaining himself with scenes and landscapes more beautiful than any that can be found in the whole compass of nature.

It may be of use to remark that in one member of this sentence, there is an inaccuracy in syntax. It is very proper to say, *altering and compounding those images which we have once received into all the varieties of picture and vision.* But we can with no propriety say, *retaining them into all the varieties;* and yet, according to the manner in which the words are ranged, this construction is unavoidable. For *retaining, altering,* and *compounding* are participles, each of which equally refers to, and governs, the subsequent noun, *those images;* and that noun again is necessarily connected with the following preposition, *into.* This instance shows the importance of carefully attending to the rules of grammar and syntax; when so pure a writer as Mr. Addison could, through inadvertence, be guilty of such an error. The construction might easily have been rectified by disjoining the participle *retaining* from the other two participles in this way: "We have the power of retaining, altering, and compounding those images which we have once received and of forming them into all the varieties of picture and vision." The latter part of the sentence is clear and elegant.

> (7) There are few words in the English language which are employed in a more loose and uncircumscribed sense than those of the fancy and the imagination.

There are few words—which are employed. It had been better if our author here had said more simply, *few words in the English language are employed*. Mr. Addison, whose style is of the free and full, rather than the nervous, kind, deals, on all occasions, in this extended sort of phraseology. But it is proper only when some assertion of consequence is advanced, and which can bear an emphasis, such as that in the first sentence of the former paragraph. On other occasions, these little words, *it is,* and *there are,* ought to be avoided as redundant and enfeebling. *Those of the fancy and the imagination*. The article ought to have been omitted here. As he does not mean the powers of *the fancy and the imagination* but the words only, the article certainly had no proper place; neither, indeed, was there any occasion for the other two words, *those of*. Better if the sentence had run thus: "Few words in the English language are employed in a more loose and uncircumscribed sense than fancy and imagination."

> (8) I therefore thought it necessary to fix and determine the notion of these two words, as I intend to make use of them in the thread of my following speculations, that the reader may conceive rightly what is the subject which I proceed upon.

Though *fix* and *determine* may appear synonymous words, yet a difference between them may be remarked, and they may be viewed, as applied here, with peculiar delicacy. The author had just said that the words of which he is speaking were *loose* and *uncircumscribed*. *Fix* relates to the first of these, *determine* to the last. We *fix* what is *loose;* that is, we confine the word to its proper place that it may not fluctuate in our imagination and pass from one idea to another; and we *determine* what is *uncircumscribed;* that is, we ascertain its *termini* or limits, we draw the circle round it that we may see its boundaries. For we cannot conceive the meaning of a word, or indeed of any other thing, clearly, till we see its limits and know how far it extends. These two words, therefore, have grace and beauty as they are here applied, though a writer more frugal of words than Mr. Addison would have preferred the single word *ascertain,* which conveys, without any metaphor, the import of them both.

The *notion of these words* is somewhat of a harsh phrase, at least not so commonly used as the *meaning of these words. As I intend to make use of them in the thread of my speculations.* This is plainly faulty. A sort of metaphor is improperly mixed with words in the literal sense. He might very well have said, *as I intend to make use of them in my following speculations.* This was plain language; but if he chose to borrow an allusion from *thread,* that allusion ought to have been supported; for there is no consistency in *making use of them in the thread of speculations;* and indeed, in expressing anything so simple and familiar as this is, plain language is always to be preferred to metaphorical. *The subject which I proceed upon* is an ungraceful close of a sentence; better, *the subject upon which I proceed.*

> (9) I must therefore desire him to remember that, by the pleasures of the imagination, I mean only such pleasures as arise originally from sight, and that I divide these pleasures into two kinds.

As the last sentence began with, *I therefore thought it necessary to fix,* it is careless to begin this sentence in a manner so very similar, *I must therefore desire him to remember*—especially as the small variation of using, *on this account* or *for this reason,* in place of *therefore* would have amended the style. When he says, *I mean only such pleasures,* it may be remarked that the adverb *only* is not in its proper place. It is not intended here to qualify the word *mean* but *such pleasures,* and therefore should have been placed in as close a connexion as possible with the word which it limits or qualifies. The style becomes more clear and neat when the words are arranged thus: "By the pleasures of the imagination, I mean such pleasures only as arise from sight."

> (10) My design, being first of all to discourse of those primary pleasures of the imagination, which entirely proceed from such objects as are before our eyes; and, in the next place, to speak of those secondary pleasures of the imagination, which flow from the ideas of visible objects, when the objects are not actually before the eye but are called up into our memories or formed into agreeable visions of things that are either absent or fictitious.

It is a great rule in laying down the division of a subject to study neatness and brevity as much as possible. The divisions are then more distinctly apprehended and more easily remembered. This sentence is not perfectly happy in that respect. It is somewhat clogged by a tedious phraseology. *My design being first of all, to discourse—in the next place, to speak of—such objects as are before our eyes—things that are either absent or fictitious.* Several words might have been spared here; and the style made more neat and compact.

> (11) The pleasures of the imagination, taken in their full extent, are not so gross as those of sense, nor so refined as those of the understanding.

This sentence is distinct and elegant.

> (12) The last are indeed more preferable, because they are founded on some new knowledge or improvement in the mind of man; yet it must be confessed that those of the imagination are as great and as transporting as the other.

In the beginning of this sentence, the phrase *more preferable* is such a plain inaccuracy that one wonders how Mr. Addison should have fallen into it, seeing *preferable,* of itself, expresses the comparative degree and is the same with "more eligible" or "more excellent."

I must observe farther that the proposition contained in the last member of this sentence is neither clear nor neatly expressed—*it must be confessed that those of the imagination are as great and as transporting as the other*. In the former sentence, he had compared three things together—the pleasures of the imagination, those of sense, and those of the understanding. In the beginning of this sentence, he had called the pleasures of the understanding *the last*; and he ends the sentence with observing that those of the imagination are as great and transporting *as the other*. Now, besides that *the other* makes not a proper contrast with *the last*, he leaves it ambiguous whether, by *the other,* he meant the pleasures of the understanding or the pleasures of the sense; for it may refer to either, by the construction; though, undoubtedly, he intended that it should refer to the pleasures of the understanding only. The proposition reduced to perspicuous language runs thus: "Yet it must be confessed that the pleasures of the imagination, when compared with those of the understanding, are no less great and transporting."

> (13) A beautiful prospect delights the soul as much as a demonstration; and a description in Homer has charmed more readers than a chapter in Aristotle.

This is a good illustration of what he had been asserting and is expressed with that happy and elegant turn, for which our author is very remarkable.

> (14) Besides, the pleasures of the imagination have this advantage above those of the understanding, that they are more obvious and more easy to be acquired.

This is also an unexceptionable sentence.

> (15) It is but opening the eye, and the scene enters.

This sentence is lively and picturesque. By the gayety and briskness which it gives the style, it shows the advantage of intermixing such a short sentence as this amidst a run of longer ones, which never fails to have a happy effect. I must remark, however, a small inaccuracy. A *scene* cannot be said to *enter;* an *actor* enters, but a scene *appears* or *presents itself.*

> (16) The colours paint themselves on the fancy, with very little attention of thought or application of mind in the beholder.

This is still beautiful illustration, carried on with that agreeable floweriness of fancy and style which is so well suited to those pleasures of the imagination of which the author is treating.

> (17) We are struck, we know not how, with the symmetry of anything we see, and immediately assent to the beauty of an object, without inquiring into the particular causes and occasions of it.

There is a falling off here from the elegance of the former sentences. *We assent* to the truth of a proposition but cannot so well be said *to assent to the beauty of an object. Acknowledge* would have expressed the sense with more propriety. The close of the sentence too is heavy and ungraceful—*the particular causes and occasions of it;* both *particular* and *occasions* are words quite superfluous; and the pronoun *it* is in some measure ambiguous, whether it refers to beauty or to object. It would have been some amendment to the style to have run thus: "We immediately acknowledge the beauty of an object, without inquiring into the cause of that beauty."

> (18) A man of polite imagination is let into a great many pleasures that the vulgar are not capable of receiving.

Polite is a term more commonly applied to manners or behaviour than to the mind or imagination. There is nothing farther to be observed on this sentence, unless the use of *that* for a relative pronoun, instead of *which*—an usage which is too frequent with Mr. Addison. *Which* is a much more definitive word than *that,* being never employed in any other way than as a relative, whereas *that* is a word of many senses—sometimes a demonstrative pronoun, often a conjunction. In some cases we are indeed obliged to use *that* for a relative, in order to avoid the ungraceful repetition of *which* in the same sentence. But when we are laid under no necessity of this kind, *which* is always the preferable word and certainly was so in this sentence. *Pleasures which the vulgar are not capable of receiving* is much better than *pleasures that the vulgar etc.*

> (19) He can converse with a picture and find an agreeable companion in a statue. He meets with a secret refreshment in a description; and often feels a greater satisfaction in the prospect of fields and meadows than another does in the possession. It gives him, indeed, a kind of property in every thing he sees; and makes the most rude, uncultivated parts of nature administer to his pleasures: so that he looks upon the world, as it were, in another light and discovers in it a multitude of charms that conceal themselves from the generality of mankind.

All this is very beautiful. The illustration is happy and the style runs with the greatest ease and harmony. We see no labour, no stiffness or affectation; but an author writing from the native flow of a gay and pleasing imagination. This predominant character of Mr. Addison's manner, far more than compensates all those little negligences which we are now remarking. Two of these occur in this paragraph. The first, in the sentence which begins with *it gives him indeed a kind of property.* To this *it* there is no proper antecedent in the whole paragraph. In order to gather the meaning, we must look back as far as to the third sentence before, the first of the paragraph, which begins with *a man of a polite imagination.* This phrase, *polite imagination,* is the only antecedent to which this *it* can refer; and even that is an improper antecedent, as it stands in the genitive case, as the qualification only of *a man.*

The other instance of negligence is towards the end of the paragraph, *so that he looks upon the world, as it were in another light.* By *another light,* Mr. Addison means a light different from that in which other men view the world. But though this expression clearly conveyed this meaning to himself when writing, it conveys it very indistinctly to others and is an instance of that sort of inaccuracy, into which, in the warmth of composition, every writer of a lively imagination is apt to fall and which can only be remedied by a cool, subsequent review. *As it were* is upon most occasions no more than an ungraceful palliative; and here there was not the least occasion for it, as he was not about to say anything which required a softening of this kind. To say the truth, this last sentence, *so that he looks upon the world,* and what follows had better been wanting altogether. It is no more than an unnecessary recapitulation of what had gone before—a feeble adjection to the lively picture he had given of the pleasures of the imagination. The paragraph would have ended with more spirit as the words immediately preceding—*the uncultivated parts of nature administer to his pleasures.*

> (20) There are, indeed, but very few who know how to be idle and innocent, or have a relish of any pleasures that are not criminal; every diversion they take is at the expense of some one virtue or another, and their very first step out of business is into vice or folly.

Nothing can be more elegant or more finely turned than this sentence. It is neat, clear, and musical. We could hardly alter one word or disarrange one member without spoiling it. Few sentences are to be found more finished or more happy.

> (21) A man should endeavour, therefore, to make the sphere of his innocent pleasures as wide as possible that he may retire into them with safety and find in them such a satisfaction as a wise man would not blush to take.

This is also a good sentence and gives occasion to no material remark.

> (22) Of this nature are those of the imagination, which do not require such a bent of thought as is necessary to our more serious employments, nor, at the same time, suffer the mind to sink into that indolence and remissness, which are apt to accompany our more sensual delights; but like a gentle exercise to the faculties awaken them from sloth and idleness, without putting them upon any labour or difficulty.

The beginning of this sentence is not correct and affords an instance of a period too loosely connected with the preceding one. *Of this nature,* says he, *are those of the imagination.* We might ask, of what nature? For it had not been the scope of the preceding sentence to describe the nature of any set of pleasures. He had said that it was every man's duty to make the sphere of his innocent pleasures as wide as possible, in order that, within that sphere, he might find a safe retreat and a laudable satisfaction. The transition is loosely made by beginning the next sentence with saying, *of this nature are those of the imagination.* It had been better if, keeping in view the governing object of the preceding sentence, he had said, "This advantage we gain" or "This satisfaction we enjoy by means of the pleasures of imagination." The rest of the sentence is abundantly correct.

> (23) We might here add that the pleasures of the fancy are more conducive to health than those of the understanding, which are worked out by dint of thinking and attended with too violent a labour of the brain.

On this sentence, nothing occurs deserving of remark, except that *worked out by dint of thinking* is a phrase which borders too much on vulgar and colloquial language to be proper for being employed in a polished composition.

> (24) Delightful scenes, whether in nature, painting, or poetry, have a kindly influence on the body, as well as the mind, and not only serve to clear and brighten the imagination but are able to disperse grief and melancholy and to set the animal spirits in pleasing and agreeable motions. For this reason, Sir Francis Bacon, in his Essay upon Health, has not thought it improper to prescribe to his reader a poem or a prospect, where he particularly dissuades him from knotty and subtile disquisitions and advises him to pursue studies that fill the mind with splendid and illustrious objects, as histories, fables, and contemplations of nature.

In the latter of these two sentences, a member of the period is altogether out of its place—which gives the whole sentence a harsh and disjointed cast and serves to illustrate the rules I formerly gave concerning arrangement. The wrong-placed member which I point at is this: *where he particularly dissuades him from knotty and subtile disquisitions;* these words should undoubtedly have been placed not where they stand but thus: *Sir Francis Bacon, in his Essay upon Health, where he particularly dissuades the reader from knotty and subtile speculations, has not thought it improper to prescribe to him etc.* This arrangement reduces every thing into proper order.

> (25) I have in this paper, by way of introduction, settled the motion of those pleasures of the imagination, which are the subject of my present undertaking, and endeavoured, by several considerations, to recommend to my readers the pursuit of those pleasures; I shall, in my next paper, examine the several sources from whence these pleasures are derived.

These two concluding sentences afford examples of the proper collocation of circumstances in a period. I formerly showed that it is often a matter of difficulty to dispose of them in such a manner as that they shall not embarrass the principal subject of the sentence. In the sentences before us, several of these incidental circumstances necessarily come in—*By way of introduction—by several considerations—in this paper—in the next paper.* All which are with great propriety managed by our author. It will be found, upon trial, that there were no other parts of the sentence, in which they could have been placed to equal advantage. Had he said, for instance, "I have settled the notion (rather, *the meaning*) of those pleasures of the imagination, which are the subject of my present undertaking, by way of introduction, in this paper, and endeavoured to recommend the pursuit of those pleasures to my readers, by several considerations," we must be sensible that the sentence, thus clogged with circumstances in the wrong place, would neither have been so neat nor so clear, as it is by the present construction.

John F. Kennedy: Inaugural Address

(January 20, 1961)

1   We observe today not a victory of party but a celebration of freedom, symbolizing an end as well as a beginning, signifying renewal as well as change. For I have sworn before you and Almighty God the same solemn oath our forebears prescribed nearly a century and three-quarters ago.

2   The world is very different now. For man holds in his mortal hands the power to abolish all forms of human poverty and all forms of human life. And yet the same revolutionary belief for which our forebears fought is still at issue around the globe, the belief that the rights of man come not from the generosity of the state but from the hand of God.

3   We dare not forget today that we are the heirs of that first revolution. Let the word go forth from this time and place, to friend and foe alike, that the torch has been passed to a new generation of Americans, born in this century, tempered by war, disciplined by a hard and bitter peace, proud of our ancient heritage, and unwilling to witness or permit the slow undoing of those human rights to which this nation has always been committed, and to which we are committed today at home and around the world.

4   Let every nation know, whether it wishes us well or ill, that we shall pay any price, bear any burden, meet any hardship, support any friend, oppose any foe to assure the survival and the success of liberty.

5   This much we pledge—and more.

6   To those old allies whose cultural and spiritual origins we share, we pledge the loyalty of faithful friends. United, there is little we cannot do in a host of co-operative ventures. Divided, there is little we can do, for we dare not meet a powerful challenge at odds and split assunder.

7   To those new states whom we welcome to the ranks of the free, we pledge our word that one form of colonial control shall not have passed away merely to be replaced by a far more iron tyranny. We shall not always expect to find them supporting our view. But we shall always hope to find them strongly supporting their own freedom, and to remember that, in the past, those who foolishly sought power by riding the back of the tiger ended up inside.

8   To those people in the huts and villages of half the globe struggling to break the bonds of mass misery, we pledge our best efforts to help them help themselves, for whatever period is required, not because the Communists may be doing it, not because we seek their votes, but because it is right. If a

free society cannot help the many who are poor, it cannot save the few who are rich.

9   To our sister republics south of our border, we offer a special pledge: to convert our good words into good deeds, in a new alliance for progress, to assist free men and free governments in casting off the chains of poverty. But this peaceful revolution of hope cannot become the prey of hostile powers. Let all our neighbors know that we shall join with them to oppose aggression or subversion anywhere in the Americas. And let every other power know that this hemisphere intends to remain the master of its own house.

10   To that world assembly of sovereign states, the United Nations, our last best hope in an age where the instruments of war have far outpaced the instruments of peace, we renew our pledge of support: to prevent it from becoming merely a forum for invective, to strengthen its shield of the new and the weak, and to enlarge the area in which its writ may run.

11   Finally, to those nations who would make themselves our adversary, we offer not a pledge but a request: that both sides begin anew the quest for peace, before the dark powers of destruction unleashed by science engulf all humanity in planned or accidental self-destruction.

12   We dare not tempt them with weakness. For only when our arms are sufficient beyond doubt can we be certain beyond doubt that they will never be employed.

13   But neither can two great and powerful groups of nations take comfort from our present course—both sides over-burdened by the cost of modern weapons, both rightly alarmed by the steady spread of the deadly atom, yet both racing to alter that uncertain balance of terror that stays the hand of mankind's final war.

14   So let us begin anew, remembering on both sides that civility is not a sign of weakness, and sincerity is always subject to proof. Let us never negotiate out of fear, but let us never fear to negotiate.

15   Let both sides explore what problems unite us instead of belaboring those problems which divide us.

16   Let both sides, for the first time, formulate serious and precise proposals for the inspection and control of arms, and bring the absolute power to destroy other nations under the absolute control of all nations.

17   Let both sides seek to invoke the wonders of science instead of its terrors. Together let us explore the stars, conquer the deserts, eradicate disease, tap the ocean depths and encourage the arts and commerce.

18   Let both sides unite to heed in all corners of the earth the command of Isaiah to "undo the heavy burdens . . . [and] let the oppressed go free."

19   And if a beachhead of co-operation may push back the jungle of suspicion, let both sides join in creating a new endeavor, not a new balance of power, but a new world of law, where the strong are just and the weak secure and the peace preserved.

20   All this will not be finished in the first one hundred days. Nor will it be

finished in the first one thousand days, nor in the life of this Administration, nor even perhaps in our lifetime on this planet. But let us begin.

21 In your hands, my fellow citizens, more than mine, will rest the final success or failure of our course. Since this country was founded, each generation of Americans has been summoned to give testimony to its national loyalty. The graves of young Americans who answered the call to service surround the globe.

22 Now the trumpet summons us again—not as a call to bear arms, though arms we need; not as a call to battle, though embattled we are; but a call to bear the burden of a long twilight struggle, year in and year out, "rejoicing in hope, patient in tribulation," a struggle against the common enemies of man: tyranny, poverty, disease and war itself.

23 Can we forge against these enemies a grand and global alliance, North and South, East and West, that can assure a more fruitful life for all mankind? Will you join in that historic effort?

24 In the long history of the world, only a few generations have been granted the role of defending freedom in its hour of maximum danger. I do not shrink from this responsibility; I welcome it. I do not believe that any of us would exchange places with any other people or any other generation. The energy, the faith, the devotion which we bring to this endeavor will light our country and all who serve it, and the glow from that fire can truly light the world.

25 And so, my fellow Americans, ask not what your country can do for you; ask what you can do for your country.

26 My fellow citizens of the world, ask not what America will do for you, but what together we can do for the freedom of man.

27 Finally, whether you are citizens of America or citizens of the world, ask of us here the same high standards of strength and sacrifice which we ask of you. With a good conscience our only sure reward, with history the final judge of our deeds, let us go forth to lead the land we love, asking His blessing and His help, but knowing that here on earth God's work must truly be our own.

The Editors of The New Yorker: John F. Kennedy's Inaugural Address

As rhetoric has become an increasingly dispensable member of the liberal arts, people have abandoned the idea, held so firmly by the ancient Greeks and Romans, that eloquence is indispensable to politics. Perhaps President Kennedy's achievements in both spheres will revive a taste for good oratory—a taste that has been alternately frustrated by inarticulateness and dulled by bombast. There have been a few notable orators in our day—most recently Adlai Stevenson—but they have been the exceptions, and it has taken Mr. Kennedy's success as a politician to suggest that the power to "enchant souls through words" (Socrates) may soon be at a premium once more. Whatever the impact of the Inaugural Address on contemporary New Frontiersmen, we find it hard to believe that an Athenian or Roman citizen could have listened to it unmoved, or that Cicero, however jealous of his own reputation, would have found reason to object to it.

We are all familiar by now with the generally high praise the President received for his first speech, but before the responsibility for a final judgment is yielded to Time it would be a shame not to seek the opinion of a couple of true professionals. Both Aristotle and Cicero, the one a theorist and the other a theorizing orator, believed that rhetoric could be an art to the extent that the orator was, first, a logician and, second, a psychologist with an appreciation and understanding of words. Cicero felt further, that the ideal orator was the thoroughly educated man. (He would be pleased by Mr. Kennedy's background, with its strong emphasis on affairs of state: the philosopher-orator-statesman.) Of the three types of oratory defined by the ancients—political, forensic, and display (in which audience participation was limited to a judgment of style)—the political was esteemed most highly, because it dealt with the loftiest of issues; namely, the fate of peoples, rather than of individuals. ("Now the trumpet summons us again . . . against the common enemies of man. . . .") The ideal speech was thought to be one in which three kinds of persuasion were used by the speaker: logical, to present the facts of the case and construct an argument based on them; emotional, to reach the audience psychologically; and "ethical," to appeal to the audience by establishing one's own integrity and sincerity. The Inaugural Address, being a variation on the single theme of man's rights and obligations, is not primarily logical, although it contains no illogic; it is an appeal to men's souls rather than to their minds. During the Presidential campaign, Mr. Kennedy tested and patented an exercise in American psychology that proved to be all the emotional appeal he required for the inaugural speech: "And so, my fellow-Americans, ask not what your country can do for you, ask what you can do for your country." His ethical persuasion, or indication of this personal probity, consisted of an extension of that appeal: ". . . ask of us here the same high standards of strength and sacrifice which we ask of you."

Aristotle recognized only one (good) style, while Cicero thought that there were three styles—the plain, the middle, and the grand. To Aristotle, who considered it sufficient for a style to be clear and appropriate, avoiding undue elevation (whence bombast) and excessive lowliness, it would have seemed that Mr. Kennedy had achieved the Golden Mean. The formality of the Inaugural Address ("To that world assembly of sovereign states, the United Nations . . .") is appropriate to the subject; the language ("In your hands, my fellow-citizens, more than mine, will rest the final success or failure of our course") is clear and direct. Cicero's ideal orator was able to speak in all three styles, in accordance with the demands of his subject, and in that respect Mr. Kennedy filled the role by speaking plainly on the practical ("All this will not be finished in the first one hundred days"), by speaking formally but directly on the purpose of national defense ("For only when our arms are sufficient beyond doubt can we be certain beyond doubt that they will never be employed"), and by speaking grandly on the potential accomplishments of the movement toward the New Frontier ("The energy, the faith, the devotion which we bring to this endeavour will light our country and all who serve it—and the glow from that fire can truly light the world").

The address, however, is largely in the grand style, which is characterized by Cicero as the ultimate source of emotional persuasion, through figures of speech and a certain degree of dignified periodic rhythm, not iambic ("The world is very different now. For man holds in his mortal hands the power to abolish all forms of human poverty, and all forms of human life"). The oration is so rich in figures of speech—the many metaphors include a torch, a beachhead, jungles, a trumpet, a tiger—that we can imagine students of the future studying it for examples of antithesis ("If a free society cannot help the many who are poor, it cannot save the few who are rich"), personification (". . . the hand of mankind's final war"), and anaphora ("Not as a call to bear arms, though arms we need; not as a call to battle, though embattled we are . . ."). "Battle" and "embattled"—an excellent example of paronomasia.

And so we leave the speech to the students of rhetoric, having invoked for Mr. Kennedy the blessings of Aristotle and Cicero, and for ourself the hope that he has re-established the tradition of political eloquence.

Analysis of the Style of John F. Kennedy's Inaugural Address

> "If, in the effective use of language, style is the man, style is the nation too; men, countries, and entire civilizations have been tested and judged by their literary tone."—John F. Kennedy

General Situation for the Speech

If we are to relate the style of the Inaugural Address to its content, we must take into account the subject matter, the occasion, the audience, and the ethos of the speaker. An inauguration is a solemn, ceremonial event, attended by certain traditions and rituals. A speech delivered on such an occasion is usually of the ceremonial variety, although there may be deliberative elements in it. What the people have come to expect is not so much a speech that lays down a specific program as a speech that sets a mood. In striking the keynote of the coming administration, the speaker will try to heal the wounds that may have been inflicted during the campaign, to remind the audience of a common heritage and a common purpose, to set forth, in a general way, the policies and objectives of the new administration, and to reassure the international community of the continuity and determination of the nation.

Since a ceremonial speech like this deals in generalities rather than in particulars, it can very easily slip off into platitude and pious cant. In seeking to please everyone with a "safe" speech, the speaker runs the risk of pleasing no one. In striving for that happy mean between the general and the specific, between the trite and the bizarre, and between the offensive and the fulsome, the speaker will have to draw on all his or her ingenuity to come up with a content and a form that will impress the audience without boring them.

Having characterized the kind of speech that is usually delivered at an inauguration, we might consider now the special situation that faced President Kennedy on that January morning in 1961. John Fitzgerald Kennedy was the youngest man and the first Catholic to be elected to the highest office in America, and he had been elected by a narrow margin of votes. His youth, his religious affiliation, and his narrow victory at the polls—all these combined to establish some doubts about him in the minds of his own people and the people of other countries. Having created an image, during the campaign, of enormous vitality and considerable political shrewdness, this leader of the New Frontier had to fulfill his promise to push the country forward. Clearly, this was an occasion when a powerful ethical appeal would have to be exerted if the confidence and initiative of the people were to be aroused.

What about the audience for this address? There would be the immediate audience—the high dignitaries on the platform and the thousands of people gathered in the plaza in front of the Capitol building. Then there were the millions of people who would see and hear the speaker through the medium of television. And finally there would be the millions of people in foreign lands who would read accounts of the speech in their newspapers the next day. Taken together, this was a vast, heterogeneous audience, posing special problems for the speaker. As we have remarked before, the larger and more heterogeneous the audience is, the more difficult it is to adjust the discourse to fit the audience. In his content and his style, the President must strike some common denominator—but a common denominator that does not fall below the dignity that the occasion demands.

Having looked at the general situation that prevailed for the speech, let us now see how the President accommodated his means to his end. In this analysis, of course, we are going to investigate only the way in which the President accommodated his *style* to the subject matter, occasion, audience, and his own personality.

The Speech as a Whole

One of the first things that strikes the reader is the relative brevity of the speech—1343 words, which at the normal rate for public address would take between nine and ten minutes to deliver. When the President wrote this speech he could not have known that the "live" audience for the speech would be standing in the biting cold that followed a heavy snowstorm in the Washington area on the day before the inauguration. So the President had not made his speech brief out of consideration for his wind-chilled audience. In preparing the speech, however, he might have taken into consideration that it would be delivered at the end of some lengthy preliminary speech-making. But perhaps the consideration that mainly determined the brevity of the speech was the traditional nature of inaugural addresses. As we have observed, inaugural addresses usually deal in broad, undeveloped gener-alizaties. Principles, policies, and promises are enunciated without elabo-ration.

Paragraphs

The relative brevity of the speech is reflected in the paragraph and sentence structure. A glance at the printed text of the speech reveals a succession of short paragraphs. Of the twenty-seven paragraphs in the speech, ten have only one sentence; seven paragraphs are two sentences long; and another seven are three sentences long. The longest paragraphs (9 and 24) contain only four sentences. In terms of averages, there are 49.3 words per paragraph and 1.92 sentences per paragraph.

The President is trying to cover a lot of ground in this short speech. In or-der to do this, he enunciates his principles, promises, and policies in a litany of capsule paragraphs. The effect of these unelaborated paragraphs would have been slight if the President had not rendered many of those paragraphs memorable by the brilliance of his style.

Sentences: Length

Descending to the next smallest unit of discourse, the sentence, we note some interesting facts about the length and kinds of sentences. The two ex-tremes of sentence length are represented by the sentence of eighty words (second sentence of paragraph 3) and the sentence of four words (third sen-tence of paragraph 20). The average length of the President's sentences is 25.8 words. But what is more revealing about the President's style is the variation above and below this average. Fourteen of the fifty-two sentences (27 percent) in the speech are ten words or more *above* the average; but twenty-three sentences (44 percent) are five words or more *below* the aver-age. Although the President has a number of unusually long sentences—66 words (paragraph 10), 64 words (paragraph 22), 54 words (paragraphs 8 and 13)—an unusually high proportion of his sentences are composed of twenty words or less. Even by modern journalistic standards, a twenty-word sentence is short. This high proportion of short sentences matches the over-all brevity of the speech and the short paragraphs. Although the President displays an admirable variety in sentence-length, his heavy use of the short sentence does suggest that he had his *listening* audience in mind when he composed his speech. Another consideration that may have influenced the President in the use of short sentences is that short sentences help to create the effect of sententiousness that is appropriate for a ceremonial speech.

Sentences: Grammatical Types

Having noted a high proportion of relatively short sentences, we might expect that a majority of the sentences would be of the simple or compound type. But a close investigation of the grammatical types reveals that this is not so. Twenty (38.4 percent) of the sentences are simple; only six (11.6 percent) sentences are compound. But twenty-six sentences (exactly 50 percent) are complex. Taken together, the simple and compound sentences constitute 50 percent of the whole, but the predominant grammatical type is the complex sentence. What this reveals is that the President manages the expansion of his sentences mainly through the sophisticated powers of subordination. A study of the sequence of sentences, however, shows how well the President has mixed the grammatical types in order to avoid monotony of structure. Only in a half dozen or so places in the speech does he string together two or more sentences of the same grammatical type.

Sentences: Rhetorical Types

When we study the rhetorical patterns of the speech, we note another interesting feature of President Kennedy's style. The predominant rhetorical structure is antithesis. This recurring structure was perhaps dictated by the fact that the speech deals mainly with comparisons of opposites (end–beginning, old–new, rich–poor, friend–enemy). He strikes the theme of the speech and the antithetical keynote in the first sentence: "We observe today *not a victory of party* / *but a celebration of freedom*—symbolizing *an end* / as well as *a beginning*—signifying *renewal* / as well as *change*." Additional examples of antithesis are not hard to find:

> to friend and foe alike (paragraph 3)
>
> United . . . Divided (paragraph 6)
>
> To those old allies . . . To those new states (paragraphs 6, 7)
>
> If a free society cannot help the many who are poor, it cannot save the few who are rich. (paragraph 8)
>
> What problems unit us . . . those problems which divide us (paragraph 15)

And the most memorable line of the speech is cast in the form of an anti-thesis:

> . . . Ask not what your country can do for you—ask what you can do for your country.

Most of these antitheses of thought are laid out in parallel grammatical structure. The recurring parallelism is appropriate here because although the President is pointing up opposites by his antitheses he wants to suggest that these opposites can be reconciled. Opposites can be reconciled only if they are co-ordinate, and one way to emphasize the co-ordinate value of opposites is to juxtapose them in a parallel grammatical structure.

The other use that the President makes of parallelism is for the purpose of specification or enumeration, as in these three examples:

> born in this century, tempered by war, disciplined by a hard and bitter peace, proud of our ancient heritage (paragraph 3)

> pay any price, bear any burden, meet any hardship, support any friend, oppose any foe (paragraph 4)

> Together let us explore the stars, conquer the deserts, eradicate disease, and encourage the arts and commerce (paragraph 17)

As we shall see when we come to study the figures of speech, there are additional schemes intertwined in many of these parallel and antithetical patterns.

Before concluding this section on rhetorical patterns, we shall point out some other features of style. If students needed any evidence to justify their use of a co-ordinating conjunction at the beginning of the sentence, they could cite this speech. The President begins fourteen of his sentences (over 25 percent) with a co-ordinating conjunction. There is, of course, ample precedent for this usage in modern prose and the prose of earlier centuries. But it is interesting to note how effective rhetorically this means of articulating sentences is in the President's speech. Let us look at just one example of this usage:

> We dare not tempt them with weakness. For only when our arms are sufficient beyond doubt can we be certain beyond doubt that they will never be employed. (paragraph 12)

Contrast the effect of this with the following:

> We dare not tempt them with weakness, for only when our arms are sufficient beyond doubt can we be certain beyond doubt that they will never be employed.

The content and rhetorical scheme of both sentences is exactly the same, and perhaps if one were *reading* the second sentence aloud, one could produce the same effect as the first sentence has. But on the printed page, a special emphasis is achieved by setting off the second clause in a sentence by itself and by signaling the syllogistic relationship of the two clauses by the capitalized initial *For*. If you analyze the other uses of initial co-ordinating conjunctions, you will usually find some rhetorical purpose being served.

Sentences: Functional Types

The overwhelming majority of the sentences are declarative. This proportion is appropriate in a speech that is designed to inform and reassure the world about the objectives of the new administration. Occasionally, however, the President uses some other functional types of sentence. In paragraph 23, he uses two rhetorical questions ("Can we forge against these enemies a grand and global alliance, North and South, East and West, that can assure a more fruitful life for all mankind? Will you join in that historic effort?"). These questions occur at the point in the speech when the President is about to launch into his peroration. Up to this point the President has been declaring what he will do, what the American people will do. Now he wants to suggest what the international community can do to support his program of peace and prosperity. But he can only suggest—he cannot dictate or predict—what other countries will do. The rhetorical questions are phrased in such a way, however, that the natural answer to them is a resounding *Yes*.

The President groups together two other types of functional sentences—imperatives and hortatives. In paragraphs 25, 26, 27 (the concluding paragraphs of the speech), we see three sharp imperatives, using the verb *to ask*, which leave the citizens with a call to action. Up to this point, the audience have been mere listeners to this ceremonial discourse. Now the audience must be engaged actively. The imperatives point to the general line of action that they must take.

The series of fourteen hortative sentences ("Let us . . . Let both sides . . .") in paragraphs 14 through 20 also lays down a program of action, but the directives are softened by being cast in a hortatory form. (The Latin and Greek languages would have used the subjunctive mood of the verb to create this effect.) The President here is seeking to induce action, not command it. In other words, he wants to persuade rather than coerce.

Diction

The diction of the speech unobtrusively but unmistakably exerts an influence on the effect of the speech. The simplicity of the diction is perhaps not immediately noticeable, but when one studies it, one notes that there is almost no word that a moderate intelligent high-school graduate would have to look up in a dictionary. A closer study of the diction reveals a high proportion of monosyllabic words: some 951 words in the speech (71 percent) are monosyllabic. In paragraphs 19 and 20, the proportion of monosyllabic words is as high as 80 per cent. Even in the peroration of the speech, where one might expect the orator to make use of the sonorous cadence that can be achieved with polysyllabic diction, one finds a high proportion of one-syllable words. This monosyllabism helps to account not only for the impression of simplicity but also for the note of strength in the speech—a note that people had come to associate with the vigor of this youthful public figure. In working over the drafts of the speech, the President must consciously have sought out simple, Anglo-Saxon words.

Having noted the high proportion of monosyllabic words, one might expect to find also a high proportion of concrete words. But this is not the case. Investigation of the nouns in the speech turns up many abstract words—words like *freedom, poverty, tyranny, loyalty, devotion, responsibility, aggression, subversion*. And most of this abstract diction is Latinate and poly-syllabic. Aside from the figures of speech—which we will investigate later—there are surprisingly few concrete words—*huts, villages, stars, deserts, graves*. Whatever air of concreteness the speech has is created by the figures of speech. Perhaps the high proportion of abstract words is the natural conse-quence of the brief, unelaborated character of the speech. Once the President had decided to enunciate only the broad, general policy of his administra-tion, it was almost inevitable that most of his substantive words would be ab-stract. What we have in this short speech really is a series of undeveloped topic sentences.

Another thing that accounts for the formal quality of this ceremonial speech is the occasional use of slightly archaic diction. We find the President using such words as *forebears* (twice), *host, anew, asunder, foe, adversary, writ*. Besides echoing the tone of Lincoln's *Gettysburg Address* ("Fourscore and seven years ago," "our fathers," "final resting-place," "hallow"), this quaint diction has Biblical overtones and a certain appropriateness to the old-new motif. The President reinforced the effect of this kind of diction by two quo-tations from the Old Testament and the folksy adage about riding the back of the tiger. The repetition of certain honorific key terms, like *pledge, citi-zens, peace* also helps to reinforce the reverential tone of the speech.

Figures of Speech: Schemes

First of all, let us look at some of the schemes—those patternings of words which represent departures from the ordinary way of speaking. Since we have already remarked about the pervasive parallelism and antithesis in the speech, we will concentrate here on some of the other schemes.

There are a number of schemes of repetition. The most notable of these is anaphora—repetition of the same words at the beginning of successive clauses. Anaphora is conspicuous in two key passages in the speech: the sec-tion (paragraphs 6–11) in which the President is making a series of pledges ("To those . . ."); and the section (paragraphs 15–18) in which the President is suggesting a course of action ("Let both sides . . ."). We have previously observed that these two sections make use of parallelism. The addition of *anaphora* to these passages performs two functions: it combines with the parallelism to mark off and emphasize the co-ordinateness of the series, and it helps to establish the rhythm of the passages. The speech has no example of the opposite scheme, epistrophe (repetition of the same word at the end of successive clauses), but it does have two examples of repetition of similar words in a medial position: "bear *any* burden, meet *any* hardship, support *any* friend, oppose *any* foe" (paragraph 4); "sufficient *beyond doubt* . . . certain *beyond doubt*" (paragraph 12).

The most remembered sentence in the speech—"ask not what your country can do for you—ask what you can do for your country"—contains a figure of repetition known as antimetabole (repetition of words in converse order). Another memorable utterance—"Let us never negotiate out of fear. But never fear to negotiate"—appears to be another example of antimetabole, but it is more accurately classified as polyptoton (repetition of words derived from the same root). Here we have different conjugates of the word *fear*—serving as a noun in the first clause and as an infinitive in the second clause. There is another example of polyptoton in paragraph 22 ("Not as a call to *battle,* though *embattled* we are")—although, as the editors of *The New Yorker* observed, there is a suggestion here too of the trope called paronomasia (play on words).

President Kennedy made sparing use of the scheme of repetition known as alliteration. There are only two instances of noticeable alliteration in the speech—"the area in which its *writ* may *run*" (paragraph 10); "to *lead* the *land* we *love*" (paragraph 27). Perhaps in accord with his personality, the President avoided frequent use of alliteration because of the soft, effeminate sound-effect often produced by this figure; the President was striving for a note of strength and vigor. One wonders, though, whether the President did not intend some sound-effect of appropriate harshness in the succession of *s* and *d* sounds in "before the dark powers of destruction unleashed by science engulf all humanity in planned or accidental self-destruction" (paragraph 11).

Let us look briefly at a few more schemes. In most of his parallel series, the President shows a preference for the hurried rhythms that can be achieved with asyndeton (omission of conjunctions)—e.g., "born in this century, tempered by war, disciplined by a hard and bitter peace, proud of our ancient heritage" (paragraph 3). The President makes little use of the scheme called anastrophe (unusual word order). In the entire speech, there is only one structure that is inverted: "*United,* there is little we cannot do in a host of co-operative ventures. *Divided,* there is little we can do" (paragraph 6). It is easy to see the special emphasis the President achieves here by placing the past participles in the initial position, even though these participles do not modify, as they normally do in this position, the subject of the main clause. One could regard this structure, however, as ellipsis rather than anastrophe. The closest the President comes to the figure known as climax is in paragraphs 25, 26, 27; but even here we have to strain a bit to find any element of rising importance in the series.

Figures of Speech: Tropes

Although the President makes rather skillful use of the schemes, he is less satisfactory in his use of tropes. There are a number of metaphors in the speech, and those metaphors represent, as we remarked earlier, the chief way in which the President introduces concreteness into the speech. But many of these metaphors—"the torch," "bonds of mass misery," "the chains of poverty," "corners of the earth," "the trumpet," "the glow from that fire"—are rather hackneyed. He achieves a little more freshness in some of his more subtle metaphors, like "iron tyranny," "destruction unleashed," "twilight struggle," "forge." Perhaps his most successful metaphor is the one in paragraph 19—"And if a beachhead of co-operation may push back the jungle of suspicion." By themselves, *beachhead* and *jungle* are rather shop-worn metaphors, but they acquire a certain freshness by being combined in a complex metaphor.

The several uses of "hands" (part of the whole) and "arms" (genus for the species) can be looked upon as examples of synecdoche, but those tropes too are fairly trite. The use of "hand" in paragraph 13—"that uncertain balance of terror that stays the hand of mankind's final war"—should be classified as an instance of personification rather than of synecdoche. Perhaps the only other expression in the speech which might be read as an instance of personification is found in the last paragraph—"with history the final judge of our deeds."

Style of Delivery

Undoubtedly, a good deal of the effect of this speech was produced by the "style" of delivery. Those who watched the inauguration ceremonies on television may recall the President's clear, crisp voice, the distinctive Bostonian accent, the mannerisms of the jabbing finger, the pauses, the inflections, the stresses. All of these features of voice and gesture helped to put the speech across; combined with the carefully worked-out style, they helped to communicate the President's message to the electorate and to the world. And perhaps it would be well for the student who has read this close analysis of the style to put the speech together again by listening to it on one of the many memorial records that were issued shortly after the President's assassination. Listening to a recording of the speech will make the student aware that this was a discourse designed for oral delivery, and it might prove interesting to note how much of the highly refined style of the speech comes through to the student once he or she has had the devices of style pointed out.

Concluding Remarks

The various stylistic devices we have been observing may be looked upon by some people as the ornamentation of the speech. These devices do "dress up" the speech, but if they are regarded as no more than ornamentation, they have failed to perform the functions that rhetoricians traditionally assigned to them. These formal devices should be one of the carriers of meaning. If the diction, the composition of words, and the figures of speech are not functioning to clarify, enliven, and emphasize the thought, if they are not exerting an ethical, emotional, or logical appeal, then indeed the style of a piece is so much sounding brass and tinkling cymbals, so much sound and fury signifying nothing.

It is not so important that the style of the speech be recognizable as the "Kennedy style" as it is that the style be seen as appropriate to the subject matter, the occasion, the purpose, and the audience. Just as Lincoln's *Gettysburg Address* was not particularly impressive to the audience who heard it in the National Cemetery on November 19, 1863, so Kennedy's Inaugural Address was not—if we may judge from the restrained applause that greeted it while it was being delivered—notably impressive to the audience who heard it in the snow-packed Capitol Plaza on January 20, 1961. It is only when we get a chance to read and reread Lincoln's and Kennedy's speeches that we realize what splendid performances they were. Only a close analysis such as we have engaged in can make us aware of the great care and deliberation President Kennedy devoted to the "expression" of his speech. So much eloquence did not come by chance. It had to come from calculated choices from among a number of possibilities.

We should now be in a better position to judge whether the President's choices were judicious. And we should be in a better position to predict whether future generations will judge this Inaugural Address to be one of the noblest utterances to issue from the lips of an American statesman.

A Paragraph by Virginia Woolf
To Be Analyzed for Style

The selection here is the final paragraph of a speech that Virginia Woolf gave to the London/National Society for Women's Service on January 21, 1931. The ad dress was later printed under the title "Professions for Women" in a collection of Woolf's essays The Death of the Moth and Other Essays (1942). *In this address, Virginia Woolf is talking about a theme that she talked about in an earlier speech in 1928, a speech that was subsequently published under the title* A Room of One's Own (1929). *In the latter half of the paragraph reprinted here, Woolf picks up on the metaphor of "a room of one's own" and carries it through to the end of the paragraph. Woolf was unquestionably in the vanguard of the feminist movement in English-speaking countries. Barbara Hill Rigney, in her article "'A Wreath Upon the Grave': The Influence of Virginia Woolf on Feminist Critical Theory" (1984), said, "She [Woolf] was the first woman writer who is also readily identifiable as a feminist critic, and her methods as well as the ideology which informed those methods, her questions and self-contradictions, still constitute the methods, the questions, and the contradictions which are the central concerns of feminist theorists today." This paragraph will be analyzed for its style. Readers might ask themselves how much of the style of this piece was prompted by the fact that this is the wind-up paragraph of a discourse that is being orally delivered to a live audience of educated women. The selection here is reprinted from* Women and Writing. *Ed. Michele Barrett, New York and London: Harcourt Brace Jovanovich, 1980, pp. 62–63.*

(1) Those are the questions that I should like, had I time, to ask you. (2) And indeed, if I have laid stress upon these professional experiences of mine, it is because I believe that they are, though in different forms, yours also. (3) Even when the path is nominally open—when there is nothing to prevent a woman from being a doctor, a lawyer, a civil servant—there are many phantoms and obstacles, as I believe, looming in her way. (4) To discuss and define them is I think of great value and importance; for thus only can the labor be shared, the difficulties be solved. (5) But besides this, it is necessary also to discuss the ends and the aims for which we are fighting, for which we are doing battle with these formidable obstacles. (6) Those aims cannot be taken for granted; they must be perpetually questioned and examined. (7) The whole position, as I see it—here in this hall surrounded by women practising for the first time in history I know not how many different professions—is one of extraordinary interest and importance. (8) You have won rooms of your own in the house hitherto exclusively owned by men. (9) You are able, though not without great labor and effort, to pay the rent. (10) You are earning your five hundred pounds a year. (11) But this freedom is only a beginning; the room is your own, but it is still bare. (12) It has to be furnished; it has to be shared. (13) How are you going to furnish it, how are you going to decorate it? (14) With whom are you going to share it, and upon what terms? (15) These, I think, are questions of the utmost importance and interest. (16) For the first time in history you are able to ask them; for the first time you are able to decide for yourselves what the answers should be. (17) Willingly would I stay and discuss those questions and answers—but not tonight. (18) My time is up; and I must cease.

An Analysis of the Style of the Paragraph by Virginia Woolf

You have just seen an analysis of a complete discourse, President John F. Kennedy's "Inaugural Address." But here we will analyze a small segment of a full discourse, the final paragraph of Virginia Woolf's address to a group of women in Great Britain.

Earlier in this chapter, there is a series of Specimen Passages for Imitation, segments of longer discourses by a variety of English and American authors. You were invited to copy some of these paragraphs verbatim, just to observe and perhaps appropriate some stylistic features of professional writers' prose. You can learn a great deal simply by copying passages that others have written. But you could learn much more about style if after copying a passage, you were to write out what you had observed about the author's style while copying it.

In the analysis that follows, we will record our observations about the style of Virginia Woolf. But we must be careful about the generalizations we make from our observation of this small segment of Virginia Woolf's published writing. We can say that the features we observed are characteristic of *this* paragraph, but we would not be justified in saying that these features were characteristic of Woolf's style as a whole. Some of the features *might* be characteristic of her overall style, but we would have to analyze a much larger portion of her prose, written over a long period of time, to be justified in declaring that same salient feature that we observed in the paragraph was characteristic of her style as a whole. But even if we would not be justified in making generalizations about Woolf's style as a whole from our study of just one paragraph of her prose, we still might observe some unusual choice of diction or arrangement of words that we could adopt for our own style. And so there would be some profit for us in writing out our observations about someone's style after copying a short passage.

In preparation for your reading of this analysis, you might want to copy Virginia Woolf's paragraph so that you could observe it more closely than you can by just reading the passage and so that you could compare *your* observations with the observations recorded in the following analysis.

At the end of the analysis, there is a statistical summary of some of the features of the Virginia Woolf passage. Some of these statistics you could not come up with simply from reading the passage or even from copying it. For instance, in reading or copying the passage, you might have observed that there is a great variety in the length of Woolf's sentences, but until you had actually done some close counting you would not be able to come up with such statistics as the average number of words per sentence in this paragraph or the actual word-count for each of the eighteen sentences in this paragraph. But if you did sense that Virginia Woolf achieves an exemplary variety in the length of her sentences, you might be prompted to count the words in each sentence to confirm what you sensed. And if you were aware that one of the weaknesses of your style was a lack of variety in the length of your sentences, you might be prompted to make a conscious effort to achieve a variety in the length of your sentences. Your compilation of statistical information about other features of Woolf's style might likewise prompt you to resolve to incorporate some of those features into your own style. But don't feel that you have to adopt all features of her style. Some features may not suit your purposes or your personality.

One observation we might make about Virginia Woolf's style in this paragraph is that she seems to have a penchant for doublets—pairs of words, phrases, or clauses. For instance, here are the pairs of *words* found in this paragraph (with the number of the sentence in parentheses following the pair): "value and importance" (4); "the ends and the aims" (5); "questioned and examined" (6); "interest and importance" (7); "labor and effort" (9); "importance and interest" (15); "stay and discuss" and "questions and answers" (17). If you look closely at these pairs, you will see that in most cases, the two words are more synonymous than different in meaning. For instance, in sentence 17, "stay and discuss" and "questions and answers" are doublets in which the two words in both pairs are different in meaning; but in all the other doubtlets, the words in the pairings are roughly or closely synonymous—"value and importance," "the ends and the aims," "labor and effort." What these synonymous pairings indicate is that Woolf seems to use doubtlets more for rhythmical purposes than for discriminatory purposes.

Moreover, of the seven compound (Cp) and compound-complex (CC) sentences in this paragraph, four of them (6, 13, 16, and 18) are bipartite—that is, they are made up of two independent clauses. (The other three compounded sentences (4, 11, 12) are tripartite—made up of three independent clauses.) Closely allied to this tendency to structure words and clauses in doublets is Woolf's predilection for parallelism (balanced clauses) and anaphora (the scheme in which the beginnings of successive clauses begin with the same words). There are three examples of these stylistic features in the paragraph: "*It has to be* furnished; *it has to be* decorated; *it has to be* shared" (12); "*How are you going to* furnish it, *how are you going to* decorate it? (13); "*For the first time* in history you are able to ask them; *for the first time* you are able to decide for yourselves what the answers should be" (16). Here again, the parallelism and especially the anaphora seem to be used primarily for the rhythms they set up.

Another prominent feature of the style of this paragraph is the split construction. The very first sentence of the paragraph has one of these split constructions: ". . . that I should like, had I time, to ask you." Here, it would be natural to keep the syntax in this order: "that I should like to ask you, had I time." Instead, Woolf starts the structure, then interrupts the normal syntax with the intervening clause "had I time," and then completes the initial structure. The effect of this splitting is to give due emphasis to the phrase "to ask you." In the natural order—see above—the clause "had I time" gets the chief emphasis.

After this first sentence, there are seven other instances of split construction: 2, 3, 4, 5, 7, 9, 15. The shortest interrupting splitter is the "I think" in 4 and 15; the longest interrupting splitters are found in 7 and 9. Sometimes—especially when the interrupters are long—the reader has difficulty in processing the suspended syntax; so you should be cautioned about over-using split constructions or about using those that involve unusually long interrupters.

Another stylistic feature that Woolf is fond of is the elliptical structure. Here are three examples of elliptical structure from this paragraph—with the understood words enclosed with brackets:

> ". . . for thus only can the labor be shared, [can] the difficulties be solved" (4)

> "With whom are you going to share it, and upon what terms [are you going to share it]" (14)

> "Willingly would I stay and discuss those questions and answers—but not tonight [will I stay and discuss those questions and answers] (17)

Ellipsis is a highly sophisticated structure, and you may want to add it to your stylistic repertory. But you should be cautioned that ellipsis is a tricky syntactical structure and that if it is not handled skillfully, readers may not be able to supply the missing words.

Some of the less prominent features of the style of this paragraph are the three sentences that begin with a coordinating conjunction (2, 5, 11) (how many of you have been told by your English teacher never to start a sentence with a coordinating conjunction?); the slightly archaic adverb *hitherto* in 8 and the "had I time" in 1, an alternative way of phrasing the subordinate clause "if I had time"; the expletive structures, which some teachers discourage students from using: "it is" (2), "there is" and "there are" (3), "it is necessary" (5); the number of monosyllabic words and of metaphors in the paragraph (see the statistical data at the end of this analysis).

Perhaps the least noticeable stylistic feature is the subtle way in which Virginia Woolf shifts from the first-person pronoun *I*, which predominates in the first half of the paragraph, to the second-person pronoun *you/your* in the second half. Starting with sentence 8, the focus is on *you*, the audience, and not until the last two sentences of the paragraph does Woolf revert to the pronoun I again. It was a clever move by Woolf to put the emphasis on the audience in the second half of the paragraph, and she achieves that emphasis simply by shifting pronouns. Another clever device was the short final sentence—the shortest sentence (eight words) in the paragraph. It was appropriate to end with that short sentence, because with her time on the podium having run out, she must abruptly cease talking.

What additional stylistic features did you notice?

Statistics on the Virginia Woolf Passage

A paragraph of 337 words and 18 sentences. Average sentence—18.72 words. Longest sentence: #3 (37 words). Shortest sentence: #18 (8 words). Number of sentences 5 words or more *below* the average—9 (50 percent). Number of sentences 10 words or more *above* the average—4 (22 percent). Number of predicate verbs in all the clauses—44:

> *to be* verbs—19 (43 percent)
> Active verbs—17 (38.6 percent)
>   Transitive verbs—13 (29.5 percent)
>   Intransitive verbs—4 (9.1 percent)
> Passive verbs—8 (18.4 percent)

Sentence	1	2	3	4	5	6	7	8	9	10	11	12	13	14	15	16	17	18
Grammatical Type	Cx	Cx	Cx	CC	Cx	Cp	Cx	S	S	S	Cp	Cp	Cp	S	Cx	CC	S	Cp
No. of words	14	27	37	25	29	14	35	15	14	9	17	15	14	12	11	28	13	8
No. of monosyllables	13	20	22	18	20	8	24	13	10	7	14	13	10	10	7	22	8	8

247 (73%) of the 337 words are monosyllabic (not a single sentence in which the majority of the words are not monosyllabic)

Split constructions: #1, 2, 3, 4, 5, 7, 9, 15

Parallelism and anaphora: #12, 13, and 16 (is #13 a comma splice?)

Ellipsis: #4, 14, and 17

Repeated words: #4 great value and importance
              #7 extraordinary interest and importance
              #11 utmost importance and interest
              #1 questions
              #6 questioned and examined
              #13 [asks two questions]
              #14 [asks two questions]
              #15 questions
              #16 them [questions]; answers
              #17 questions and answers

Metaphors: #3 path, phantoms and obstacles looming
          #5 doing battle with obstacles [mixed metaphor?]
          #8 rooms in house
          #9 pay the rent
          #11 room
          #12 furnished, decorated, shared
          #13 furnish, decorate
          #14 share

Index

CPSIA information can be obtained at www.ICGtesting.com
Printed in the USA
BVOW03s0452091213

338473BV00002B/24/P